ALSO BY JAMES J. CRAMER

Confessions of a Street Addict

YOU GOT SCREWED!

WHY WALL STREET TANKED AND HOW YOU CAN PROSPER

JAMES J. CRAMER

SIMON & SCHUSTER

NEW YORK   LONDON   TORONTO   SYDNEY   SINGAPORE

SIMON & SCHUSTER
Rockefeller Center
1230 Avenue of the Americas
New York, NY 10020

SIMON & SCHUSTER and colophon are registered trademarks
of Simon & Schuster, Inc.

Designed by Jan Pisciotta

For information about special discounts for bulk purchases,
please contact Simon & Schuster Special Sales:
1-800-456-6798 or business@simonandschuster.com

Manufactured in the United States of America

10   9   8   7   6   5   4   3   2   1

Library of Congress Cataloging-in-Publication Data
is available.

ISBN 0-7432-4690-X

Acknowledgments

I want to acknowledge three fantastic inspirations for my work as an author: Suzanne Gluck, my tireless agent, David Rosenthal, whom I regard as the ultimate partner for someone who wants to tell the truth as he sees it, and Bob Bender, who is the best editor I have ever had, and I have had a lot of them.

And I can't forget America's greatest publicist, Aileen Boyle.

To Tom Clarke, the excellent chief executive officer of TheStreet.com, who allowed my dream to become a reality;

To my friend Eliot Spitzer, who did more to clean up Wall Street than any other regulator in history;

And to Karen Cramer, who explained to me years ago that Wall Street was just a giant promotion machine.

Contents

Part One

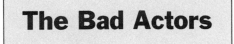

The Bad Actors

One

What Happened?

"Stocks for the Long Run . . . Buy and Hold . . . Next stop, Dow 36,000 . . . Stocks as the only asset class worth owning . . . Tech Blue Chips . . . Stocks always come back . . . Don't ever sell . . . Selling's for losers . . . Why not put Social Security into stocks, after all they are the safest investments . . ."

Ahh, that litany, that rock-solid litany of reassurance about equities. Is there a soul on the planet who didn't suffer from the multiple brainwashings that the media, the academics, the brokerage houses, and the mutual funds mercilessly beat into our heads for a decade? Amazingly, after trillions were lost, we still have no regrets, no apologies, nary a *mea culpa* from those who heartlessly led us to the financial slaughter that outranks even those of the nightmare generations 1973–1974, and, alas, 1929–1934—that's right, the Great Depression. These one-note charlatans would, even after every penny of life savings had been lost, still recite their bogus mantras meant to take our eyes off the ball, and our wallets, even as they suffered not a penny for their admonitions. They haven't learned a thing about the havoc they have wrought. They are still out there shilling their wares, except now they are saying that the stock market is *even* more undervalued than before. Dow 36,000? You better hope they've perfected cryogenics by then. That's the only way you will live to see it.

This book is meant not as an epitaph to your hard-earned savings, but as an epitaph to their cynical reassurances and pseudo-scientific claptrap. This book should serve as an antidote to their sweet nostrums that have separated you so viciously and silently from your money. In short, they thought that if they got you in, you would never get out, and they would make fortunes off you before you figured out what the heck happened to your nest egg. The charlatans wrote their assurances of ever-higher stock prices when the market skyrocketed daily. Now that it has nosedived, their il-logic seems deceitful if not downright larcenous.

Oh sure, the temptation to demonize seems far-fetched to some, particularly those who need stocks to go higher to make a living or have a successful venture. But as someone who has worked in the money business for more than three decades, and compounded money in his own fund at 24 percent after all fees, someone who has seen it all and done it all when it comes to stocks, I can tell you that exorcising demons may be the only way to assure you that it doesn't happen to you again.

Why were the odds stacked so against the individual in-vestor? Why was the bloodletting so incredibly worse than it would have been if the sole cause of the downturn were the economy? Put simply: money, greed—there was so much money to be made simply by keeping you in the dark about the practices of Wall Street. There were fees to be taken by managing assets; there were underwriter fees, initial public offering fees, fees from advertisers, mainly mutual funds and brokers; there were fees from lobbyists, accounting fees, lawyer fees, and fees from publishers. There were returns, outsized returns, that no one wanted to give up, including the public itself, and there were those huge gains that insiders generated by selling common stock against their options at the very top of the market and long after, enabling them to take out billions upon billions of dollars in gains, some right before their companies collapsed, leaving workers and pensioners holding nothing, not even a bag. The sums appropriated were so fabulous, and the penalties for abuse so small that the temptation to rig individual stocks and even the market itself, in the name of earnings "management" simply grew too great for all but the most holy of chief executives, which, alas, turned out to be too few to be noticed or to matter to battered 401k's. What started as a few apples turned into the whole orchard, but no one in a responsible position in government wants to admit that harsh but true judgment.

The actions taken by the federal government subsequent to the prodding by elected officials such as Eliot Spitzer, the attorney general of New York, who got the ball rolling, certainly helped clarify the conflicts, and even shed harsh light on the most revolting of them. But within weeks of these actions, the complex of interests that kept you in the dark about how the stock market really works was right back in action.

Which is why you need this book and need it now, because if you are going to rebuild your nest egg or fix your 401k, you first need to understand which forces destroyed it. Only then, once you understand the subtle means by which you were fooled into coughing up vast sums, will you be in a position to work your way back to where you were, *regardless of the overall market's direction*. It won't be quick—after all, those overnight methods were what got us in this mess. Rebuilding your investments may not even be exciting, but we should have left the excitement for the ballpark or the movie houses. I will recommend to you a steady, solid way to make things back that can't be corrupted by the cavalier forces that coalesced into the current brutal bear market for stocks.

First, though, let's slay those nasty villains, those bear enablers that allowed the ursine capital destroyers to roam just about anywhere they wanted and take from you with reckless abandon. This will be a difficult task, but I intend to help you make your paycheck and your retirement money grow, not shrink, and I don't want your fees, your commissions, or your capital gains. I just want your losses to stop and the capital appreciation to begin.

Two

The Forces That Took Your Money: WorldCon

If there was one defining moment of the era of shameless capitalism, it was the revelation of a $4 billion fraud—later revised to $6 billion—by WorldCom, the second-largest phone company in the United States. Sure, Enron springs to mind as precursor to all that went bad with corporate governance, but it was WorldCom, with its blatant manipulation of numbers, that caused people to realize that the whole game may, indeed, have been rigged. To a great extent, WorldCom was one of the stocks in the World Series of investing, and like the Chicago "Black" Sox of 1919, WorldCom was cheating in this World Series, and you were the loser. Everyone owned WorldCom; heck, my dad owned Worldcom because of its merger with MCI Communications. WorldCom wiped out billions upon billions of bond and stock monies. WorldCom encapsulates everything that went wrong, and everything that could still go wrong. That's because, despite the best efforts of Washington, the con that WorldCom turned into could still be played again on unsuspecting folk who believe in the worth of both common stocks and the words of the executives behind them.

We know how it all ended, with the announcement on CNBC that a giant fraud had been perpetrated on shareholders and bondholders and lower-level employees, all of whom thought that WorldCom was doing fairly well at the time of its financial demise. But how did it begin? How did it get so dirty—and how come we couldn't tell?

For that you have to go back to the mid-nineties, when Jack Grubman, the world's most famous telecom analyst, decided to elevate a phone company salesman, Bernard Ebbers, into a telephone god. Grubman, who made fortunes for investors during the long-running bull market, became the single most important player in the hottest space: telecommunications. He, above all others, was responsible for the trillion-dollar morass that telecommunications spawned, because he was the chief proselytizer for unrelenting, ineluctable, telecommunications growth. (At least until August 2002, long after the boom had turned to bust, when he left his analyst job at Salomon Smith Barney "by mutual agreement.") Grubman recognized, before all others, that there was a monumental opportunity to consolidate an industry that had been broken up by the Justice Department years and years ago and then further altered by the Telecommunications Act of 1996, which made it easy for any joker with a three-page business plan to get billions of public dollars to crack into the phone business. Grubman saw it all coming, and he had his fingers in almost all of the pies, from Global Crossing and Qwest—he was a huge backer of both, and some would say, was actually running these companies from his office in New York—to the now defunct Winstar and Teligent and, of course, the biggest con game of them all, WorldCom.

I knew Jack Grubman when he had just broken in as an analyst with Paine Webber in the late 1980s, after he left AT&T as an analyst. He and I were both Philly kids, and we liked each other instinctively. At that point Jack even helped me understand that AT&T was a loser's game and that the competition would eat its lunch. It was a great call and he dined on it for years, until he was noticed by Citigroup's Salomon Smith Barney and became not just their analyst, but also their deal-maker, the man behind the scenes who couldn't wait to revolutionize telecommunications in this country.

At Salomon Smith Barney, Grubman pioneered a method of combining, in one office, the investment banking, stock research, stock distribution—he controlled a lot of hot deals—and prognostication of a whole industry. Grubman was not content with just telling you which stocks were worth buying and selling; he wanted to create new companies, run them, sell their stocks, and then merge their stocks, each time taking giant fees from everyone involved. What's giant in a business where people routinely make hundreds of thousands of dollars a year? How about $20 million a year! He was the highest-paid man on Wall Street, making even more than his boss, Sandy Weill. He deserved it, if the criterion isn't how right you are, but how much business you bring into a firm. And in the 1990s that was the only litmus that mattered.

But there was a problem with all of this business, an ethical problem that nearly everyone on Wall Street turned a blind eye toward: Grubman was a walking conflict of interest. In fact, he seemed to flaunt these conflicts, always preferring the larger corporate finance side over the retail investor, because the corporations paid bigger fees than retail ever could. You could say he overdosed the financial world in telecommunications. He had plenty of help doing it, though, as he became a celebrity analyst lauded by his firm, the industry he promoted, and the media, which made him the public face for what was hot on Wall Street. Should someone at Salomon Smith Barney have stopped Grubman from playing the role of deal-maker, operator, critic, and seer? Sure, but there was simply too much money to be made to get in Grubman's way. At the peak, in the late 1990s, getting a call back from Grubman meant the world, maybe the sun and all of the planets that revolve around it.

In the mid-1990s, Grubman met up with a perfect foil in Bernard Ebbers, a mean-spirited telephone salesman from Mississippi who viewed virtually everyone in the world with contempt, except Jack. Ebbers decided that he wanted to put together the largest phone company in the world and Grubman was going to be his banker to get there. Even though WorldCom was public, with a board of directors and auditors who were meant to check Ebbers, or at least provide some oversight, Bernie Ebbers ran WorldCom as if it were a private fiefdom, and sometimes I wondered if Grubman was his only confidant. Ebbers carried World-Com around in his back pocket. Wherever he was, the company was, and he let you know it. Constantly.

To make all of these acquisitions and to consolidate the industry, WorldCom needed a highly valued stock, a "currency" as we call it on Wall Street. To get a highly valued stock you needed promotion. Stocks that aren't promoted by Wall Street brokerage houses don't go up. You need strong buys and super-duper buys and rosy scenario-spinning to encourage large institutions and the public to bid your stock up. Given the dowdy nature of the phone business, only acquisitions could create the kind of sizzle to get things rolling for WorldCom. Grubman hyped the stock to the moon and then presented a constant stream of companies for World-Com to purchase with the "full faith and credit" of Jack Grubman behind it. Grubman printed a lot of currencies at his peak, including Global Crossing, which Jack had assisted in taking over dowdy old Rochester Telecom—another old and steady outfit that was ripped to shreds during the era—and Qwest, which Jack had helped to buy an undervalued Baby Bell, U.S. West.

Targets and acquirers were plundered under this rapacious system, but not before tons of stock could be sold and tons of fees taken into the hype that Jack created. After deals closed, Jack raised his earnings estimates of the acquiring company, so the stocks could rally again and new targets could be lined up for picking off. It was a beautiful thing to watch: Each time that Grubman touted WorldCom, the firm's network of retail and institutional salespeople would get on the horn and book huge orders in the stock, which would give WorldCom an ever-higher currency. After he made the call, he would then appear on television or be written about in the newspapers as the man with the hot hand. Then others, not part of the Smith Barney universe, would propel the stocks ever higher after they heard about the calls. No one was ever critical of Grubman, or complained that he might actually be working more for World-Com than for you—we later found out that he was busy attending WorldCom meetings and crafting day-to-day strategies. Instead, they simply bought in to the excitement.

The principal means of levitation by which companies could be propelled involved earnings manipulation. Grubman, as well as many other worshipful analysts, began to play a parlor game with the earnings estimates of the companies they followed, of which WorldCom was the best example. WorldCom would create earnings estimates that could be beaten handily. Then, of course, because the targets were set low, those estimates were trumped when the quarters were announced.

Why did beating the Street—topping the earnings estimates—mean so much? Because another key player in the greed era, the mutual funds, bought into the process lock, stock, and barrel. For most of the twentieth century, pension funds were the largest owners of stocks. But, in the 1990s, with the advent of defined contribution plans handled by individuals, not the companies, mutual funds became the largest purchaser of stocks. They also became the biggest movers of stock prices. As mutual funds proliferated with the creation of the mass 401k, the talent pool of seasoned managers couldn't keep up with the growth. Nor could their managers find enough cheap stocks to own. The number of funds and the wealth of assets outstripped the system's ability to produce prudent risk-takers. Firms instead hired young mutual fund managers who had never seen a bear market, not even a serious correction. These inexperienced turks, in order to justify their portfolios, embraced brand-new metrics that could justify buying and holding stocks at any cost and at any price levels. They had to come up with some self-fulfilling, outlandish metrics because without "New Economy" parameters they would have been forced to sell stocks as they became overvalued by traditional benchmarks. If these new managers of the new economy had cared about traditional methods of valuations, which showed stocks going well beyond any reasonable method of valuation in the late 1990s, then they would either have to stop buying stocks or send back the money to fund investors. But that would be antithetical to these New Economy stock managers, because they were paid only by the percentage of assets. Nobody in America administers his own pay cut. So, rather than valuing stocks by means of dividends and historic price-to-earnings data, these funds embraced the "beat-the-Street estimates" that the analysts pushed on them. That methodology, would, theoretically, allow you to own stocks "for the long run" as long as they somehow managed to do better than what Wall Street expected. That way stocks that might have been worth millions, could be worth hundreds of billions, because they "beat the Street's estimates" by as little as a penny a share. And why not trust the new method of valuation? It was a theoretically objective standard created by the collective minds of highly paid analysts. It would create a hurdle that would separate good companies from bad. It was something so easily understood and followed that the media quickly embraced it and started running "earnings estimates" to be beaten. A whole industry sprang up to monitor these numbers and assess who beat them by the greatest amounts.

But what those who lived or died by this earnings momentum analysis didn't tell the public, was that the fix was in from the day this "method" began. The numbers that had to be beaten were arrived at beforehand. The mutual funds were thrilled as long as they owned these companies, of which WorldCom became the poster boy. And why not? If you only cared about whether a company beat the Street, what did it matter if a company sold at 10 times earnings or 50 times earnings or 100 times earnings—or 100 times sales for that matter. As long as the Street could be beaten—and it could be easily beaten given the acquisitions that World-Com kept making—the mutual funds could buy more WorldCom with comfort. Every few quarters WorldCom would make a major acquisition of another phone company. Given the latitude of the accounting profession, World-Com could take charges on each acquisition—not cash charges but bookkeeping charges. These were nonoperating losses, sometimes totaling in the billions. As there was no cash outlay, these "losses" could regularly be added back into earnings whenever needed to "beat" the numbers. So-called honeypot accounting allowed WorldCom and hundreds of other companies to keep making numbers long after the businesses faltered. If you couldn't make the numbers at the last minute, you could rely on your friends at investment banks to create some phony piece of business that could be reversed next quarter when things had gotten better.

No one in the market questioned this "beat the Street" methodology; in fact, everyone bolstered or abetted it. World-Com's accountants, Arthur Andersen, far from playing the role of cop on the beat, meticulously checking and double checking to be sure that the numbers reported truly did beat the Street and represented the true picture of the business, took an entirely different tack. Andersen, rather than be adversarial, sought to be a willing partner to unfettered growth, even suggesting untraditional ways, through its considerable consulting effort, to make those numbers, whether by hook or, of course, by totally blessed crook. Can't make the number? Andersen will find a way to make the number for you through financial legerdemain. And why not? How else could Arthur Andersen partners make a decent living and be in the room with titans like Ebbers if they were simply doing auditing work? All of the Big Five firms priced their auditing business at a loss in order to get in the door to be able to do more lucrative consulting business. (I saw this firsthand as a director of TheStreet.com, which was audited by Andersen. Once in, these folks had dozens of ways to augment revenues and earnings for the more compliant managers out there. When I called this farce to the attention of the viewing and listening audience, the response of Arthur Andersen was swift: they said they would fire TheStreet.com as a client unless I shut up. I didn't and they did; quite a badge of honor in retrospect.) The accountants could generate millions more dollars in consulting work if they dropped the adversarial role and instead played the role of friendly adviser. So they did it. In spades. Consulting turned into the driving business for the increasingly rich accounting firms. So what if standards had to be compromised to keep the consulting fees coming.

The media loved the "beat the Street" process, too. It was so simple, an easy way to explain why stocks went up or down. Companies either beat the estimates or failed to beat the estimates. Those stocks that went down had obviously

failed to beat; those that went up, did beat. Those that did
nothing just met the estimates. The media, eager to explain
the business world in a quick, black-and-white shorthand
way, willingly featured the analysts who participated in the
charade but said nothing about how the charade worked. As
in sports, there were winners and losers, determined by who
trumped or got trumped by the estimate machine. The
magazines and newspapers did the same, treating these
people, including Jack Grubman, as objective purveyors of
numbers, and not the insiders they really were. Why not?
These folks could talk to us on television and radio between
ads, and it didn't hurt the advertising effort, either, to have
these people on, looking and sounding intelligent and dis-
tinguished.

The mutual fund managers loved it, too. They would
talk about how they liked certain stocks like WorldCom because they had earnings "momentum," the code word for
being able to beat the earnings estimates. The mutual fund
managers loved the free exposure of television—it was the
cheapest marketing method—and those that most recklessly
pursued the highest returns got the most airtime. They were
able to raise the most money, which they then used to im-
prove the value of their stocks through endless hyping. It
was a cycle that helped propel WorldCom and other stocks
like it ever higher, long after the stocks should have been
sold by the rational stewards of your dollars.

The mutual fund managers were thrilled to find one-
decision stocks like WorldCom, where they had to do no
real thinking. And the media loved stocks like this one, too,
because it was widely held and closely followed by millions,

including the wealthy people who were monitored by Niel-son, the judge of audience ratings systems. It didn't hurt, by the way, that WorldCom was also a huge advertiser! Nobody minded that you couldn't find out much about how WorldCom was really doing, which was a good thing given how little information Bernie Ebbers was willing to share with shareholders. No matter—Jack Grubman would fill anyone in who would listen that all was going well. Periodically, when the stock would dip, he would get on his squawk box at Salomon Smith Barney and "reiterate his buy," perhaps with the added spice of a quick earnings-estimate bump of a penny or two a share—whatever was necessary to keep the stock going in the right direction. New buyers would be brought in, and the stock could go high enough to buy more competitors. It was this fertile combination that enabled WorldCom to trade at $60 a share in 1999. It seemed to be able to go on forever, particularly because of all of the honey stored up from the honeypot charges Ebbers and Grubman took on the acquisition of MCI.

Alas, all good things come to an end, though, and in 2000, with the gains of MCI now digested, and the one-time charges reversed back into the earnings stream to make sure WorldCom beat the numbers, WorldCom sought to buy Sprint. The Justice Department, fearing too much concentration—and not playing any role in the company's earnings game—decided to block the acquisition. Without the new acquisition, WorldCom was at the mercy of the actual industry pricing, which was godawful because of all the competition that Jack Grubman had bankrolled. WorldCom could no longer beat the estimates that had been created.

The string of "in-the-bag" earnings came crashing to an end. Or at least it did in the real set of books inside the company.

But Scott Sullivan, the enterprising young WorldCom chief financial officer, had other plans. Fresh out of acquisitions to shield the lackluster ongoing performance, which suffered because of cutthroat competition in the industry, Sullivan devised new means to beat the Street. He allegedly began hiding expenses or turning them into capitalizations, which don't count against earnings, to make it seem that WorldCom was making a lot more profit per revenue dollar than any other phone company. A dollar in WorldCom revenue would generate maybe two to three times the profits of anyone else in the industry, as other phone company executives looked at WorldCom's margins in awe. That suited the mutual fund investors just fine. They loved rising margins more than any other method of profitability because such margins showed that Ebbers could get the most out of a lean infrastructure. WorldCom looked *a lot* more profitable than it really was.

WorldCom was, in many ways, the victim of the other successes of Jack Grubman. The jack-of-all-trades analyst helped bring to market fistfuls of competing telephone companies, all of which were nipping at the heels of World-Com and taking away clients by offering superfast, super-low-priced services, courtesy of the incredibly cheap capital that Grubman raised for them.

As the industry's pricing began to collapse all around WorldCom in 2000, Grubman kept raising earnings numbers, not on the revenue growth, which had peaked, but on the strength of those made-up margins and fraudulent sales.

Grubman has denied any knowledge of WorldCom's wrong-
ful accounting. Unfortunately, the bogus accounting kept
institutions and individuals in the stock who would otherwise have sold it, and allowed many insiders to continue to
bail out of their stock and stock options at vastly higher
prices than they could ever have gotten otherwise. The in-
creased "cash flow," a number heretofore thought to be
"unriggable," also allowed WorldCom to repeatedly come
to the fixed income market to raise capital. In fact, World-
Com became one of the largest issuers of all kinds of bonds,
and a major holding in many of America's largest pension
plans, which needed liquid securities that paid big coupons
to fulfill their long-term mandates. The fees on the billions
of dollars in fixed income securities dwarfed even those
on the equities. These astronomical fees kept Citigroup and
Grubman well-compensated even as the stock began to de-
scend rather quickly, dropping from the 50s, to the 40s, the
30s, and ultimately through the 20s to the teens.

No matter. When the string of acquisitions in telco
came to a forced end, WorldCom, at Grubman's suggestion,
moved aggressively to the Net, snapping up hosting companies to go with its Internet backbone, UUNET, which was
meant to absorb the declining long-distance business that
had been WorldCom's bread and butter. By golly, that
"Com" in WorldCom's name wasn't just for show! World-
Com, Grubman claimed, was to be a major player in the
dot-com business, too! It was going to be the support system for the biggest thing since electricity was discovered.

In 2001, phone industry competition grew so intense
that even Grubman, who had never met a telco company he
didn't like or didn't think would grow to the sky, had to

scale back his estimates of growth. Of course, the dot-com business had peaked by then, too, and the backbone to the Net was generating hundreds of millions in losses, not gains. That didn't become obvious, though, until Salomon's gigantic retail client base was riddled with WorldCom. With the stock down by two-thirds, the bogus earnings kept shining right on through. Now Grubman could pitch World-Com as the ultimate *value and* growth stock. As its sickening slide steepened, buyers and shareholders contented themselves with the knowledge that WorldCom had plenty of cash to ride out whatever storms might lie ahead, courtesy of all of those financings Grubman had orchestrated. The stock slid into the single digits in late 2001 and seemed to settle there for a while, although for several months, with each Federal Reserve easing, Jack pitched the stock as a great way to play the rebound.

It was during this prolonged slide that Ebbers proved his show-business best—and worst! As the stock was sinking into the 20s and teens, he would appear at investing forums, which had become a regular feature of the bull market, and attack anyone who would differ about the great growth prospects of his company. Ebbers would brag that not only did the critics know nothing, but that he was buying his own stock hand over fist as they should be doing. Because he had made a lot of money when the sun was shining, these buys shocked no one. But the sheer size of them, their immensity, did make people sit back and think, Hmmm, that Bernie's one shrewd guy, he must have something big up his sleeve. That insider buying, up to $300 million worth, kept the balls in the air even as other phone companies started to shrink as their bankrolls disappeared.

Of course, the buys turned out to be one more part of the illusion. They were made with loans from the board of directors that Bernie controlled. The $300 million he used to make a "statement" with his buys, required Ebbers to risk *nothing*. It was OPM, other peoples' money. Ebbers was using WorldCom as his own private bank, even though it was a public company and no one on the board, including the current CEO, John Sidgemore, objected.

Even as the stock drifted down to the low single-digits, the charade continued. The company expressed full confidence about its finances and Grubman ratified that belief every single time. With the stock at 2, though, even this board couldn't take Ebbers's total unaccountability and booted him. Grubman stuck by the stock to the bitter end, downgrading it only after it hit 90 cents.

Of course, the very day after the downgrade, the largest single corporate fraud in history was discovered. John Sidgmore, who served as Ebbers's chief operating officer, and took $6 million in fees from WorldCom in 2001, discovered the $4 billion accounting fraud that later became $6 billion. Scott Sullivan, the chief financial officer, who, of course, had chosen Florida as his place of residence to build a $17 million mansion—untouchable in bankruptcy because of Florida's liberal homestead exemption—resigned when it was discovered that he had dramatically overstated earnings for at least five quarters and maybe as many as eight. No wonder the rest of the industry was so jealous! It turns out that a dollar of revenue at WorldCom was worth no more than a dollar of revenue anywhere else, after all! It was all done with accounting mirrors. Anyone with an accounting background should have been able to see what was wrong, but because so many people were involved in covering it up, the sleight of accounting hand went undetected.

Immediately, all of the cash was gone as creditors panicked and stopped advancing the firm money. Instead, they demanded instant repayment before any more services could be advanced. WorldCom, which was supposed to have billions in cash and reserves, filed for bankruptcy protection with almost no cash on hand. All of those financial statements that had been ratified by the auditors, and touted to the mutual funds and the media turned out to be meaningless. The cynical folks at Nasdaq allowed the common stock to keep trading for weeks as if it were worth something. It will surely be wiped out in bankruptcy because of the company's gigantic debt load. The debtors will inherit the company. And so the WorldCom story abruptly ends, taking with it an incredible amount of life savings, in exchange for which we got to see Sullivan and his assistant led away in handcuffs as his lawyer shouted that the arrests were "political" in nature.

Where were the regulators during all of this? Where was the SEC, to put a stop to all of the incredible hype and lies? "Not my job," the SEC seemed to be saying. As long as WorldCom filed its filings on time—regardless of what it said on them—the government could do nothing but watch. After all, it is not the SEC's role to rule whether stocks are too expensive or cheap. That's supposed to be Wall Street's role, the role of the bankers, the accountants, the lawyers. In this case, it was totally corrupted by the gigantic fees that WorldCom delivered. And it isn't the SEC's role to snoop around and find out if something might be dirty at WorldCom. The agency has been so starved of funds by both Republicans and Democrats alike that it doesn't have the manpower to prosecute out-and-out fraud even when that fraud is delivered on a silver platter, let alone the kind of arcane stuff that WorldCom lied about. The SEC would have okayed a leaf named WorldCom if it had blown through the window.

Where were the lawyers and investment bankers who should have seen this stuff coming when they checked off on the myriad financings WorldCom did? Who the heck cared? Why get in the way of a fee-generating juggernaut. The numbers looked fine to everyone. The media couldn't be counted on to find it either; if you hinted that something was dirty, your managing editor was right in your face telling you about corporate libel.

Jack Grubman remained unrepentant throughout, acknowledging only that perhaps he had misjudged the growth of the industry. That was his shortcoming—he was too optimistic! He denied that he had any inside knowledge of the fraud when he downgraded the stock to a sell at 90 cents.

One has to wonder about the timing of Grubman's $100,000 check to the Democratic Party. On Capitol Hill, soon after the Democrats received his check, Grubman vigorously protested his innocence about the new information that drove the stock from 90 cents to 30 cents the next day. Apparently, the highest-paid analyst on Wall Street failed to see the real irony, that he failed to catch not the 60 cents lost in the day after he downgraded it, but the 60 dollars lost over a two-year period that he stood by this sham of a company.

Feel conned? You should. This fraud, with all of its witting and unwitting accomplices, may have single-handedly created more distrust of the market and may have eroded more confidence than any other failure of the era. But it was no more ingenious than dozens of other cons that went on simultaneously as other companies took advantage of the laxity in the system.

Three

Enron

In the last half-dozen years the democratization of the market proved positively viral in its spread. The government enabled 55 million people to handle their own finances. Or, more accurately, they "forced" people to do it because previously companies were in charge of making sure that these people had pensions for retirement. Individuals, in essence, became their own portfolio managers for their IRAs and 401k's. The public thought it knew all it had to know, as stock research went online and organizations ranging from The Motley Fool to E*TRADE made it seem so easy that you felt foolish if you didn't do it yourself. All you had to do was buy "good stocks." What were good stocks? Well, whatever you thought were good stocks were good stocks *provided you held them for the long term.* Any stock could be a good stock, as long as it traded!

A combination of holding stocks—any stocks—for the

long run, as Wharton's Jeremy Siegel came wrongly to stand for, and a belief that if you liked the product a company made—a bastardization of a model proselytized by Peter Lynch, the best stock picker ever to come out of Fidelity—you should own the stock, created a giddy sense that you couldn't lose in the market. Buying and holding the stocks of companies that made valuable parts in your personal computer made sense. Buying and holding the stocks of companies that installed fast phone lines made more sense. Buying and holding the stocks of the parts that the phone installers used made the most sense of all. That's all you needed, that knowledge and a modem, and you were in the portfolio business, *just like the pros.*

Homework consisted of watching CNBC and asking others if they liked the products as much as you did, something that could be done unscientifically on the Web, through chatrooms, or "scientifically" by asking your neighbor or the guys you hung out with.

We all cheered the democratization of stocks because, like elections, voting for the stocks you like by owning them just had to be a good thing. Democratization, however, did not bring with it all the skills you needed to make good judgments for the long term. For example, no one provided the tools of how to read a balance sheet or assess cash flows. No one taught people how to spot red flags or how to tell if a company wasn't doing as well as you thought. And no one explained that stocks, particularly tech stocks, were high-risk pieces of paper and that the real long-term value of stocks came from dividends as much as capital appreciation—and most of the tech stocks didn't have dividends. Those experts who tried to raise such questions were never given airtime. That would have been too risky because they might just knock the subtle, tacit compact between advertisers and offstage executives that it was un-American to say anything negative about the value of stocks or the increasingly dim quality—that is, dishonesty—of earnings that beat the Street.

But commentary might not have mattered anyway. The accountants, particularly Arthur Andersen, which had audited the books for Sunbeam and Waste Management—two high-profile wrongdoers that never suffered criminal sanctions and therefore had little moral suasion on potential bad actors—had come up with new, ingenious, ways to disguise how poorly companies were doing. And the bankers, eager to accommodate the accountants and earn giant fees, weren't about to say no. They loved crafting intricate dodges that, for million-dollar fees, made companies look much better than they really were. They hid debt and hid liabilities but showed all of the assets you needed to be enticed into buying stock. They bragged about their prowess in being able to fool the debt-rating agencies and the few skeptical reporters. They touted their ability to gussy up dowdy balance sheets or put lipstick on a pig, making the financials look prettier than they were. Hence, the "off balance sheet" terrors were born.

No company finessed off-balance-sheet activities as well as Enron. No company hid more bad businesses than Enron. No company took advantage of more laws and halfhearted attempts by regulators, stripped of authority by lobbyists paying off Congress, than Enron. The executives at Enron had transformed a sleepy gas pipeline company into a hard-charging behemoth that made markets in everything from

BTUs to water—and at a huge profit, or so it seemed. In reality, Enron was making next to nothing legally.

The New Enron with all of its New businesses, from trading energy to trading water, was just a huge con game that everyone—the accountants, the lawyers, the press, and the government—blessed. It was a game that was many years in the making. Unlike WorldCom, which lied about its financials and was a simple accounting fraud, the story of Enron is a tale about trashing the government's ability to help us spot fraud and deceit. It is about taking apart the radar that the federal government has built up since the last time we had sustained chicanery, in the 1920s and 1930s.

In the 1920s, utilities used their huge reach and clout to combine with each other and move into deregulated businesses, where they could gouge the consumer. They became giant trading companies that pyramided business on top of business to create behemoth equity structures that eventually bankrupted all who touched them.

Because of those flagrant abuses, the U.S. government put in place a series of regulators and regulations that would forbid people from taking advantage of utilities again to abuse the public. The government established the Securities and Exchange Commission to guard against stock abuses, the Commodity Futures Trading Commission to guard against manipulation in the futures market (by forcing companies to put up their own capital so they wouldn't risk it with harebrained schemes to monopolize power), and the Public Utilities Holding Commission to make sure that utilities couldn't use their monopolies to screw consumers and exploit the public. They also developed the Federal Energy Regulatory Commission to be sure that the utilities didn't keep power away from certain areas to drive up the price of electricity or gas. All of these rules made energy companies less attractive to Wall Street, causing their stocks to languish and their executives to lag behind most others in compensation.

Enron changed all of that. Enron, through donations and through powerful representatives in Congress, including Senator Phil Gramm, who championed every single Enron initiative, managed to take out every piece of radar that the government had set up to avoid manipulation on a grand scale. Enron's minions relaxed any enforcement possibilities, giving the management at Enron free rein to make up revenues and profits. And they did.

The SEC? Enron made sure that its filings were so difficult to understand that the SEC didn't even take the time to examine them. The Commodities Futures Trading Commission's mandate that lots of money be put up before a company could trade? Gutted by Enron, which also put the former chairwoman of the organization, Wendy Gramm, wife of Phil Gramm, on its board. Enron had no margin requirements whatsoever and had to put up very little capital to trade, even though any other company doing what it did would have had to risk lots of its own capital to stay in the game.

The Federal Energy Regulatory Commission? Aggressive lobbying by Enron emasculated the FERC and made its regulators toothless. The commission looked the other way as Enron amassed a trading system that allowed it to create shortages of energy wherever it wanted to and then deliver energy at higher prices to take advantage of those shortages. It was the electrification grid version of highway robbery.

Public Utility Holding Commission? Enron got an exemption from it so it could expand beyond utilities, the very thing the agency was created to prevent. Every single entity that could enforce, inspect, or keep Enron honest was sidetracked or mooted by Enron. This was a deliberate destruction of all of the safeguards of our capitalist system and it took hefty donations to both parties to pull it off.

More important, Enron knew how to play the game. It knew that if it were the biggest commission or fee generator, it would get its way on Wall Street and with its accountants. Wall Street would praise its every move and drive its stock relentlessly higher so stock could be sold and millions of dollars be made by Enron executives. Enron paid Arthur Andersen, its auditors, millions of dollars in consulting fees to look the other way. It paid Vinson & Elkins almost as if it were an investment bank, instead of a law firm, and the firm checked off on everything Enron did.

It gave more money than almost any other firm to both Democrats and Republicans, so no regulator felt safe scrutinizing the company. And if someone, anyone, spoke negatively about it, this company knew how to get its way. Enron even went after John Olson, the terrific, honest Merrill Lynch analyst who was fired for being negative about Enron.

Which is why it should come as no surprise that Enron immediately took on far more debt than it could sustain, not being regulated by the Public Utility Holding Commission, and abused derivatives to raise billions off the books because the Commodity Futures Trading Commission blessed anything that the firm did. It is not surprising that Enron tried to hide as much as possible in special-purpose entities that it knew no one would ever examine because, what the heck, they were bought and were going to stay bought.

For the longest time, the company was able to generate lots of good gains simply by running a trading room in which it could figure out where power was most needed and then keeping power out of that market so it could extort windfall profits, as it did in California. But when the federal government stepped in—despite all of Enron's lobbying efforts—and broke up the stranglehold Enron had on power in California, the company was no longer able to meet Wall Street's estimates. Given that the executives wanted to sell millions of shares at high prices, something that could only be done *if* there was a higher-than-natural stock price, the company had to find other ways to book gains.

So, among other things, which may have included getting Merrill Lynch to create fictitious profits at the end of 2000—a claim Merrill Lynch denies—Enron chose to sell shares in companies that had just become public, even though the SEC strictly forbade such sales for new securities. No matter, Enron just sold the stocks to an entity controlled by the chief financial officer and booked a profit to make its numbers. When the stocks later started falling apart, hurting the secret entity they were sold to, Enron simply transferred millions upon millions of shares to the entity to make it solvent.

Of course, all good things have to come to an end. When Enron's stock started plummeting as people became aware of both the self-dealing and the duplicitous management, the scheme to defraud both the public and *the company* itself broke down and the company collapsed from both its hidden debt and the hidden shares that it owed.

It was only after we saw the extent that Arthur Andersen had abetted the fraud, and, worse, moved to shred documents about the fraud, that we realized that Enron might not be an isolated incident. One by one, all of the power traders, such as Dynegy, Mirant, Reliant, and Williams, started collapsing, and with them came lots of other stocks that had hitherto been strong, including the banks and the brokers that had loaned money and prestige to these operations.

Who was really at fault with Enron? Was it Ken Lay, who masterminded the dismantling of the federal radar meant to pick up scams like Enron? Was it Jeff Skilling, who created the Byzantine structure of Enron and quit the company when it fell through $48, perhaps because that's where so much stock had to be issued to back up the venture capital bets gone awry? Was it Andy Fastow, who represented the entities that took the venture capital positions off of Enron's book in return for millions of dollars in fees? Was it the board, including Wendy Gramm, who looked the other way as the executives were allowed to self-deal and steal shareholders blind? Was it the brokers, who facilitated the corrupt structures that fell apart overnight and fired or punished anyone critical of Enron because Enron was the biggest bill-payer on Wall Street? Was it Arthur Andersen, the allegedly independent auditor that never seemed to disagree with anything that Enron did to evade the shareholders' ability to make critical judgments about the books? Was it Vinson & Elkins, the law firm Enron dominated, which refused to take seriously the complaints of whistle-blower Sharon Watkins and checked off on bogus partnership after bogus partnership? Was it the mutual funds, which bought this stock all the way down to $1 and defended it endlessly? Was it the SEC, which didn't have the time or inclination to challenge any of the ridiculous finances that Enron presented to it? Was it the fault of the media, which repeatedly embraced Enron as the most progressive company around? Or was it Congress, which eagerly looked the other way whenever Enron greased its palms? Or maybe it was just everyone because Enron represented, not a simple fraud like WorldCom, but a wholesale breakdown of every aspect of the legal, accounting, governmental, and regulatory bulwark meant to keep corporate America honest. In short, Enron had rigged the system like no other company, including the grotesque villains of the 1930s. The collapse of Enron will be the chapter in the history book that explains how crony capitalism spun out of control in the United States at the turn of the twenty-first century. Oh, and as in so many other corporate scandals, not a single dime was ever recovered and returned to its rightful owners, you.

Four

Rhythms Net

The most egregious method by which you got screwed by Wall Street was not WorldCom or Enron. It was the boom stocks, stocks like Rhythms Net Connections. Chances are, you might not have heard of Rhythms, a real firefly of a stock—some would say a tsetse fly—that appeared in 1999 and went belly-up less than two years later. It never made a profit—in fact, it lost hundreds of millions of dollars—yet at its peak, it had a market cap of $7 billion.

How that happened, and how that demonstrated Wall Street at its worse, *totally driven to take away your money* for the privilege of big fees, has never been explained, until now. Rhythms Net was one of those companies that arose from the moronic 1996 telecom deregulation act, which spawned $3 trillion in new enterprises that would later fail. Congress meant the act to give more competition to the regional Bell operating companies. It did, but the companies that were created didn't have enough capital or customers to see it through. They were, for the most part, shams that were meant to be bought by other phone companies after they got some critical mass.

Rhythms Net Connections, for example, was supposed to be able to take on Verizon, BellSouth, and SBC Communications, which were dragging their feet to install high-speed lines to your home. The company, jam-packed with allegedly wise ex-regulators, thought it could game the system by taking advantage of the right provided for in the act to allow outside contractors to install high-speed phone lines in the "local loop" or last mile. In other words, this company was a glorified telephone installer that passed itself off to the stock market as a state-of-the-art telecommunications play. Great costume and makeup work! It simply couldn't be resisted by a market that was brainwashed into thinking that anything telecom was high-tech and worth investing in.

Rhythms played squarely on the cynicism Wall Street showed toward both the dot-com movement and those retail investors who played it. The bankers and the investors in Rhythms, as well as the executives, must have known that the company was losing fortunes as it came public, and there was little reason to expect that it would generate fortunes for years. But they also knew that one of the main reasons that people were installing high-speed phone lines was because they wanted to trade stocks over them. The audience for Rhythms's product was the same as the audience that clamored for the on-line initial public offerings and "invested" with the electronic brokers like E*TRADE. The company's executives and the bankers knew that the Net-happy retail customer base wouldn't be able to resist a fast-line-phone play, even one that was bathed, swathed, and boiling in red ink. The greatest fun of investing came from buying stocks on-line that helped you trade on-line faster.

And who were the bankers behind it? None other than Jack Grubman at Salomon Smith Barney and some no-names at Merrill Lynch. And who were the largest investors? None other than the venture capital folks at Enron. I told you this one was at the intersection of everything bad.

Because of the way the government regulates IPOs, the bankers knew they had a hot deal on their hands, one that would come to a giant premium. They knew it because they offered only a very small sliver of the total stock outstanding, which kept demand much tighter than it would have been otherwise. They offered just enough to get the retail investor juiced into buying the stock on-line the day of the offering but not so much that it wouldn't go to a ridiculous premium immediately and be the talk of the businesss press for days.

In April of 1999, Rhythms sold 9.38 million shares to the public at a price of $21. Of course, most of those shares went to large institutions that were big commission generators at Salomon Smith Barney. Some of those shares went to "friends and family" of Rhythms, which we discovered later, were also friends of Jack Grubman. Salomon doled out stock freely to the likes of Bernie Ebbers and other telecom cronies.

The significance of friends-and-family stock? You are able to flip it at the opening. It has no trading restrictions. That meant that when Rhythms opened at $56, the friends were free to sell it, having "paid" $21 a share. That's a profit of $35 for nothing—and it is not clear that the friends even had to put up capital to receive the stock. They also might have sold at $115, where Rhythms traded less than a week later. Others, including many insiders, were "locked in" and couldn't sell, rules that pertained to Enron, too. But this friends-and-family allowance permitted the buddies of Salomon to make a fortune with no risk whatsoever because they bought in at the initial public offering price of $21. They made millions in windfall for no effort with nothing on the line. It smacked of a bribe, a kickback, to continue to do business with Salomon Smith Barney. Sweet.

Alas, the executives at Enron didn't like the fact that they had to wait, in some cases, at least a year to be able to sell their stock to the open market. (The SEC has strict rules governing insider sales, to make sure that they can't flood the market. Consequently, someone like me, who was worth $360 million on paper the day TheStreet.com came public, had no ability to realize that gain without breaking the law.) Enron didn't like having to play by the rules that other insiders lived by. It wanted to take advantage of the huge run-up in price generated by retail, and it didn't care about the laws that said it couldn't.

Andy Fastow, the CFO of Enron, in particular, didn't like being at the market's mercy. He had to know, like everyone else involved with the company, that business was hitting a wall *even as the company came public* because the dot-coms were hitting a wall and the customer base wasn't developing at the pace that Rhythms originally expected. He knew that Rhythms was losing hundreds of thousands of dollars every day it was in business because the installation costs for each line were running much higher than Rhythms expected. (The installers had to come back multiple times because of the complexity of the high-speed lines. It was never a good business.)

So what did Enron's Fastow do? He booked the profit on Rhythms anyway, even though he was legally bound not to, to help Enron make up for hideous losses elsewhere. He needed to do that to keep Enron's stock high, so the executives could dump Enron shares willingly to the clueless public, something that Enron execs did *every single quarter.* Enron sold Rhythms to LJM Partners, an entity controlled by Andy Fastow, who reportedly received $30 million in management fees (LJM being the initials of Fastow's wife and kids). LJM later refinanced the purchase through another special purpose entity (SPE) called Raptor. This group made its money by selling Enron puts, where $48 (the Enron stock price) was the breaking point. Of course, LJM didn't have any money to pay for the stock, so Enron gave the entity the right to some Enron stock to pay for the Rhythms Net Connections. It had to do this because no bank or broker in the country could allow this transaction to occur, so in essence Enron created its own currency, Enron dollars, if you will, to pay for taking Rhythms off its books at a great profit. Enron dollars were like Geoffrey dollars at Toys "R" Us, but not as convertible.

Of course, Fastow couldn't just give the stock to Raptor. That would be too easy and too fraudulent even for him because it would require registering the stock, which would expose his scheme to the glare of the public, and not just the obtuse board of directors. Fastow took advantage of the fact that Enron's board didn't understand derivatives—even though board member Wendy Gramm was the head of the

CFTC, which regulates them—and to finance the buy, he had Raptor sell puts—or options to sell at a later date—against Enron struck at $48, puts that would be worthless if the stock went higher but would be a huge liability if the stock went lower. Given all of the lengths to which Enron was willing to lie, distort, and steal to make the numbers good, it didn't seem possible for its stock to go down. In other words, Fastow let this bogus entity that he controlled make a bet that Enron wouldn't go below $48, and it took the money it got for selling those puts on Enron and used it to buy the Rhythms stock from Enron in a totally illegal transaction! Everything would work out fine as long as Enron's stock stayed high. No one would ever know that the reason why Enron made its numbers and allowed the pump-and-dump scam to continue was that it had a phony gain on the sale of Rhythms.

Of course, if Enron's stock dropped below $48, then the company (by way of LJM) would have to issue cash to cover the busted bet. Confused? You are supposed to be, just as the jury that gets this case will be confused, which, again, is something the clever Enron fraudsters knew ahead of time. One of the reasons it is taking so long to prosecute Enron is that every step it took was designed to, if ever discovered, be too difficult for juries to understand. Why commit simple fraud when you can commit complex fraud that can't be understood by 99% of America's juries?

Is it any wonder that about the time Enron stock struck $48 on the way down, the chief executive officer of Enron, Jeffrey Skilling, who must have known about the Rhythms deal and where it would come unglued, bolted ship, citing family concerns? You can be sure Skilling wanted no part of a deal crafted under his watch that was about to unravel.

Enron managed to get a great price for its Rhythms. But LJM got the stock in free fall and the exposing of this ruse is what caused Enron to have to restate its books. Even though Arthur Andersen, the accountants, and Vinson & Elkins, the lawyers, blessed this venal transaction, and the board made a special exception for it, Fastow and friends couldn't hide the fact that Enron had booked a big gain in Rhythms but that a related entity now had a giant loss in Rhythms. This little phone installer, and the transaction that was designed to beat the lockup laws that we mortals have to live by, is what brought down the whole edifice of America's seventh-largest company.

Within less than eighteen months after Rhythms came public, what Enron and the brokerage folk knew all along, that the company had a failed business model, was now obvious to the hapless public that had bought the stock. The company filed for bankruptcy. Ahh, and that is where things came full circle, as WorldCom's Bernie Ebbers, one of the few people to make a profit on Rhythms from his flip when the company came public, got the nod from Jack Grubman to purchase the remaining good Rhythms assets out of bankruptcy to make WorldCom into more of a Net play. In September of 2001, WorldCom bought Rhythms for peanuts. Anyone who bought the IPO when it opened and held on to it got nothing. Those who later bought and held Rhythms also got nothing. Only the flippers, the insiders at Enron, and of course, the CEO of Rhythms, who sold $10 million of stock as soon as she was legally allowed, were able to make big money from this fiasco. The biggest winners? Jack Grubman and Andy Fastow—and Grubman pal Bernie Ebbers—who each made millions—Grubman in fees directly from Rhythms and Fastow from LJM—for all of their hard work promoting and selling the short-lived Rhythms Net Connections. Grubman and Fastow made fortunes; the rest of us got stuck holding the Rhythms bag.

Part Two

The Failed Philosophy and Institutions

Five

All-Stocks-All-the-Time

How did we get to be such suckers to begin with? How did we let the Grubmans and the Fastows and the Ebberses get their way with us? How did we become so lacking in skepticism about a process so fraught with risk and chicanery? For a long time, investors had accepted the fact that stocks were risky investments. In 1991 when I helped start *Smart Money,* the Dow Jones–Hearst cooperative venture, we debated how much exposure people should have to the stock market versus other assets. We talked about the notion that maybe, just maybe, people should have more stocks than bonds at ages like fifty or fifty-five. We thought that with people living longer and working longer, the traditional "out of stocks into bonds" equation that everyone recommended to investors over fifty, might not apply anymore. We argued that stocks had a place in the portfolio even as late as your seventies. It was heresy, pure heresy, at a time when stocks were still considered to be heartbreakers that could take away your breath and your money in a flash.

I thought that my former teachers at Goldman Sachs would brand me a lightweight or an eccentric with such an injudicious equity allocation. The market had crashed not once but twice in the four years before the magazine started, and stocks were cutting peoples' lungs out. But I had a bullish outlook, especially on technology equities, and believed that you had to put more money in stocks than had been previously recommended. I saw that the United States was taking back manufacturing leadership from the overextended Japanese and that our software and semiconductor and personal computer firms were in ascendance. So we went with an allocation that included stocks for septuagenarians and kept people largely in equities until their fifties.

Not long after that "bullish" allocation, the great technology bull market began. Our allocation, overnight, went from seeming risky to seeming prudent. In fact, those who did not participate in the nineties bull market, such as Jeff Vinik, who resisted by overweighting Magellan, the largest mutual fund, in bonds, not stocks, in the early 1990s, began to fall far behind the averages, which seemed to be levitating daily. In fact, the most seminal change in mutual funds had to be the sacking of Jeff Vinik, one of the great investors of our time, for being too cautious and holding both cash and bonds instead of all-stocks-all-the-time. The message from Fidelity, the best mutual fund house, was clear: you can lose your job for having too much cash but not if you own too much stock; even the worst of stocks was better than the best of bonds for mutual funds. It was in this era also that the notion of stocks "for the long term" was invented, including a text by Jeremy Siegel, the Wharton School professor, of the same name. This theory held that as long as you held on to stocks—any stocks—you would do better than with bonds. You just *had* to. Of course, what people left out of this equation was that you have to own the right stocks, ones with good dividends and balance sheets. That was the fine print. The message most investors recalled was that stocks beat bonds no matter what. So get long stocks and forget bonds.

Fueled by 401k contributions, the market took off. Investors, not just young investors, but investors of all ages, grew comfortable with the notion that not only should stocks be the predominant asset, perhaps they were the *only* justifiable asset for those with a long-term perspective. My notion of having some stocks in the later years seemed quaint only five years later. It was stocks, all-stocks-all-the-time. Before 401k's, companies created defined benefit plans that they shepherded themselves. Most of the money went to bonds, because that way the employers would be able to meet their obligations in the future without worry. You could plan your liabilities and invest accordingly in bonds without taking on the risk of a nasty equity decline, one that should be expected every few years.

Without the large pension funds, and buttressed by best-selling academic texts that demonstrated that stocks always worked best, ordinary investors began to accentuate equities, then go all equity. Then, in the mid-1990s, when some mutual fund managers with the most aggressive growth portfolios put on the best numbers, people got comfortable with portfolios composed entirely of growth equities, ones that paid no dividends. In the final phases of the stock mania, in the late 1990s, investors assembled hypergrowth portfolios with companies that were "New Economy," unconstrained by traditional valuations, business models, profits, or even ethics.

After all, fund managers who embraced the wildest growth stories reveled in the best numbers, gaining gigantic percentages quarter to quarter. Those with the best numbers then were profiled in magazines and on television as young hotshots not bound by conventional fuddy-duddy stocks. Those who embraced the most exciting concept stories were rewarded with outsized performance that led to more cover stories and more TV appearances.

That uncritical praise from journalists led to more money pouring into high-tech and New Economy funds. Those funds then invented new "reasons" to stay long, expensive stocks, reasons the brokers were more than happy to provide at the cost of additional commissions to them. Rationales, alibis, for owning the hottest of the hot. These managers became folk heroes, with the likes of Janus Fund, Putnam, Invesco, and Berger, the most aggressive shops, becoming the gold standard because of their shoot-the-lights-out returns, which dazzled the everyday investor. These funds represented the new thinking in mutual funds, the thinking that said, You give us your money, we give you the most octane, go the fastest, and get you there with the most money. It was a pitch steeped in greed, and it couldn't be resisted.

By 1997, the notion of being in anything but high-tech equities, regardless of the investor's age, seemed downright foolish—that's how outsized the returns were. The mutual funds were anxious to pile into any company that could beat the numbers consistently. Mutual funds advertised that the most aggressive holdings were suitable for retirement accounts. Anybody who said otherwise was viewed as a cantankerous throwback to an era that had long since ended. Of course, this pressure to be or look like a growth stock then gripped corporate America because the mutual funds, the marginal buyers of stock, were only interested in consistent growth.

The mutual fund industry's predilection for growth forced all but the managers of the most cyclical of stocks to embrace the mantra of earnings management. This bizarre business philosophy insured that companies beat their own projections. Through much of the mid-1990s, companies, particularly tech companies, massaged and pushed earnings to arrive at sleep-at-night numbers that made companies appealing to mutual funds, because they "met" the numbers. This game worked because there was just enough growth in the system, notably from technology and telecommunications, to keep people excited about the prospects.

It was at this point, in 1997, that two forces converged to make tech stocks the *only* stocks in peoples' portfolios: the Internet and the Telecommunications Act of 1996. These two tidal-wave forces created giant new markets that many companies could take advantage of. They gave tech, which had always been viewed by the experts as cyclical and not worthy of long-term bets, a new veneer, that of the "blue chip." This is when Americans decided to heck with the Cloroxes and the Procters—they could own the EMCs and the Suns and the Ciscos. They didn't need the slow-growth

companies anymore. Heck, they didn't even need diversification. They just needed the diversification of owning all
of the parts of the personal computer. Investors became
convinced that if you owned Dell, Intel, Microsoft, and
EMC you were completely diversified! There were so many
growth markets: the Net, e-mail, cellphones, converging
markets of entertainment and high-speed phone lines. And
with these trends came colossal investments: AOL and Amazon, Nokia and Motorola, Cisco and WorldCom . . . the list
went on and on.

Perhaps the single most exciting moment came in 1996
and 1997 when for the first time, the public became comfortable buying stocks over the Internet. Until stock-buying
came to the Net, you had to interact with people to buy
stock and you often had to pay exorbitant commissions.
Stock-buying had required a body, a human, to take an order, and humans to process the order, mail the order, tally
the order, and debit the order. The human, by the way,
could also act as the "brake," the person who might say,
"Whoa, Nellie, this one is way too risky."

Now, via the wonders of the Net, no other humans
needed to be involved. With the popular texts and the media now emphasizing that stocks were the only asset class,
you could buy them on the Web for a fraction of what it
would cost otherwise. There were no barriers to keep the
public from being fully invested. The brokers certainly
weren't going to put up any barriers, not when commercials
began to trumpet the instant riches that you could make
on-line. The academics already had bought in. The research
analysts were busy raising numbers, and the companies
themselves were thrilled with the turn of events. What was

YOU GOT SCREWED! 51

not to like about this new investor class who were able to do it themselves, to participate in some weird home-game version of what had been going on at institutions and among rich people for years and years? The electronic brokers told us that what mattered wasn't which stock you bought—they all went up; what mattered was how fast you bought them. Speed of execution trumped judgment or stock selection. And nothing was faster than buying stocks on the Internet.

Of course, the Federal Reserve wasn't too happy about the masses entering the market without the tools or guidance to pick good stocks, but it turned a blind eye as people began to borrow money—first small sums, then astronomical amounts—to purchase stocks on margin. Fed Chairman Alan Greenspan complained about "irrational exuberance," but even he eventually bought in to the New Economy. Instead of slowing raising interest rates, or at least boosting margin rates, to cool off the public's unrestrained enthusiasm, he was satisfied periodically to state that the public was buying lottery tickets masquerading as stocks. But before long everyone was already in the pool and over their heads in stocks. No other branch of government spoke out, either. People were having too much fun.

The beleaguered SEC had no complaints at all; the chairman was busy hosting brothers Tom and Dave Gardner, the Motley Fool, the jester-costumed fellows who never met a stock they didn't like and believed that tech-investing was some sort of psychological and financial imperative. They were a terrific trio, the Gardners and Arthur Levitt, encouraging everyone to believe that the playing field was leveled and they had a good chance to beat the pros in trading or investing. So what if the SEC didn't have the funds to hire the people it needed to scrutinize all of the offerings coming down the pike or spot-check the financials now that "earnings management" seemed to be the rule, not the exception. So what if the SEC could spend only cursory moments looking at the filings of the older companies like Enron or WorldCom that were trying to dress themselves up as New Economy plays. With the likes of hundreds of new companies coming public, who had time to look at what the old ones reported? As long as everyone was making money, what's the deal? The mutual funds loved it, as they were raking in money after a couple of excellent years. They were the biggest beneficiaries and darned if they were going to start worrying about whether their souped-up portfolios were suitable for their clients. Heck, the prospectuses made it clear in their 7-point type that things could get a little dicey with stocks now and then. That was enough warning for the public.

Those professionals who shrank at the prospects of paying 30 and 40 times earnings in 1997 seemed downright antediluvian when 1998 brought companies priced at 50, 60, and 70 times earnings. Mutual fund graybeards, unwilling to play, were retired to the bench, as the youthful analysts took over and recognized that they were in a new era. Now you could pay much more for stocks than ever before because, well, stocks were better and companies were much more productive and the business cycle seemed cured of downturns by the wonders of technology, which didn't need a strong economy to prosper. Remember, as long as companies beat the estimates by a penny or two, and analysts could raise numbers, the mutual funds were justified in buying much, much more with each "better-than-expected" report. The mutual funds reveled in taking down 10, 20, 30, 40 million shares of their favorite stocks and then moving them up at the end of every quarter or even every month to get more good press and attract even more money after the press featured the managers' prowess.

With the Web expanding and the Telecommunications Act greenlighting new phone companies, Wall Street began to take notice of the need to have many more phone lines as the Net expanded, one for the DSL, one for the wireless, and one for the home. Venture capitalists, sensing a terrific opportunity, created phone companies overnight to sate the demand and then created companies that made equipment to sell to phone companies and companies that installed new phone lines. This telecommunications cohort became the new favorite of all of the hot funds.

Amazingly in 1998, a setback in the bond markets, initiated by the malfunctioning of a hedge fund, Long-Term Capital Management, caused the Fed to cut rates dramatically and pump money into the system. The beneficiaries of lower rates were still another new group of stocks, the dot-coms. As Yahoo, America Online, and Amazon rose to incredible heights, venture capitalists and entrepreneurs huddled with investment bankers to meet the demand, the endless demand that seemed to come from on-line traders. Amazon, Yahoo, and AOL became the role models for literally hundreds of stock offerings not long after that, all of which had the same "beat the estimates" model. This was the moment when we fell into the total abstraction of buying stocks because they beat the estimates *even when they were losing fortunes,* a methodology that meant nothing to stock-hungry mutual funds. We started buying stocks that lost "only" 80 cents per share when we thought they were going to lose 90 cents! We started valuing companies on the basis of how their revenues were growing, not their earnings.

The confluence of all of that pumped-in money, the ease with which people could buy stock on-line, and the supply of new companies that were created to meet demand washed away all historical precedent. By the end of 1998 we were beginning to buy stocks as a multiple to *potential eyeballs,* to heck with revenues or earnings. With the spectacular CBS MarketWatch deal, which came public at $19 but opened at $90, institutions realized that the public didn't have a clue what it was doing. Dot-com mania was peaking. The banks figured out that the people who read Market-Watch are the "voters" who would pay anything for anything because they simply believed. They believed that stocks had to go up. They believed that the Net was transformational and would put anyone anchored in bricks and mortar out of business. Nobody at the investment houses could afford to stand in the way of this juggernaut, given all of the underwriting dollars at stake. Bankers began to persuade old brick-and-mortar companies like Barnes & Noble, the New York Times, and Disney to develop tracking dot-com subsidiaries to raise money to help fend off the upstarts.

Nobody cared, and few even knew, that the electronic brokers, none of which had much of a back office to process all of the orders they got from the millions of people now trading, simply handed off their orders to a behind-the-scenes firm, Knight/Trimark. That "wholesaler" then batched all of the orders into one big market buy order and opened the IPOs wherever it wanted to. Often, it shorted the stocks to the fleeced public that thought it was getting in on the ground floor. The public was getting in at the penthouse! Knight, an outfit that didn't even exist a few years before, would open up stocks wherever it pleased because the unsophisticated public used "market" orders instead of limit orders. Knight/Trimark became one more behind-the-scenes villain that may have cost you money if you ever bought a stock electronically on opening day of a new offer. The firm's windfall profits, of course, stayed with its founders. No one ever returned a dime to you for this brazen rip-off.

That batching of orders, which the brokers didn't tell you about, led to the incredible first day pops that made no one but Knight/Trimark money. Knight opened stocks absurdly high, then immediately sold their positions to the public at a substantial profit. After that the stock underwent a sickening slide. Almost every dot-com except Internet infrastructure plays, and business-to-business plays, collapsed. The two dot-com sectors just mentioned became the major focus of the investment houses. They kept rallying because the analysts repeatedly touted them, including Henry Blodget, the Merrill analyst later betrayed by his own e-mails about how he might just have to tell the truth about the crap he was pushing if the corporate finance overlords didn't get off his back. It was essential to the big year-end bonuses on Wall Street that the analysts keep the Internet juggernaut going even as the economy was a wall rising in front of them.

Most institutional people who played the game at its highest level knew that the fix was in and these stocks would tumble. But the public didn't get wind of it until long after the corrupt bargain had collapsed. In fact, the public trusted the investment-banking analysts and looked to them for guidance. They didn't understand that these analysts were simply shills, just reiterating their buys to make possible the borrowing and refinancings that produced huge profits for their firms. These analysts could be relied upon to come on television regularly and talk up the merits of these companies without ever having to admit that the fix was in and they were just trying to keep them alive long enough for insiders to sell out of their positions. The public, of course, thought the analysts were independent critics. No one let on otherwise. It was not until the attorney general of the State of New York revealed the conflicts of interest by releasing the e-mails behind the charade that the public realized it had been had and had but good. Those "independent" queens and kings of the Internet were simply trying to appease the corporate finance people who paid their salaries, not enlighten the public.

In 1999, the Fed, aware that the public was buying stocks with reckless abandon, and margining itself to the hilt, felt conflicted because of fears, vastly overblown, that Y2K would freeze the banking system. It made credit readily available to stem the Y2K worries, even as it raised rates, causing the boom to continue right into 2000. The Nasdaq put on 3,000 points virtually overnight. The investment bankers couldn't print enough stock, and the insiders were still restricted from selling because of lockups. The price gains were breathtaking, and the insiders, locked up because they couldn't do the Fastow sham trades, began salivating for the days when they were no longer bound by restrictions and could freely sell.

In the spring of 2000, the insiders, worried that they

would see these beautiful gains slip out of their grasp, began to overwhelm the market with their after-market sells. Even as they told us that their companies would one day rival Microsoft in size, they were dumping stock into the crowd. This was when Microsoft passed General Electric in market cap, only to be passed by Cisco. Cisco had a market cap of $500 billion, much larger than any other company, even as it sold at an outrageous 100 times earnings. Who cared? If it could beat the numbers, the mutual funds would play their part and move the stock ever higher.

By 2000, almost a hundred companies were capitalized at $50 billion on the Nasdaq. (There are only seven as of Fall 2002.)

Alan Greenspan, finally sensing a bubble like the one in Japan where the public grew so enamored of equities that people borrowed up to their eyeballs to buy stock, only to see stocks plummet by 80% over ten years, suddenly panicked in the spring of 2000. The market would have rolled over by itself, but he had to push it and push it big. He gave us a rapid-fire jack-up in rates and tightened money once the Y2K crisis passed. That simply sped up the monster amount of equity supply to hit the market, because companies wanted to get to market fast—too fast for the market to absorb—before capital dried up. The market, which once meant the New York Stock Exchange, now had become the Nasdaq. It went into a freefall. The beginning of the meltdown was upon us. Of course, we didn't know it at the time, and there were days, many days, when it looked like the market was going to turn. The cheerleading TV commentators told us every day that this was the day when tech would lead us back to Nasdaq 5,000.

The media, once so vigilant, played a cheerleader role during the period. It wasn't just television. *Forbes,* which had always prided itself on its skepticism, succumbed almost lock, stock, and barrel to the sirens of technology. It hired George Gilder, who put a pseudo-intellectual shine on Global Crossing, Qwest, and WorldCom in his columns. Watchdog? How about lapdog?

But the public was ill equipped to handle the downturn. Almost immediately, the mutual fund and brokerage minions were on the tube and in print telling you to stay the course, that stocks should never be sold, that selling now, at Nasdaq 4,000, no make that 3,000, no make that 2,000, would leave you in cash, and cash was trash. It was wrong to sell, you would never get back in, stocks had to reverse, they just *had* to.

The brokerage houses, which housed nary a bear at the top, reiterated that the values were there for the long-term. Analysts, unwilling to see the ballgame end, reiterated their buys. But it seemed that everyone who could own stocks already owned them and there was no one to sell them to!

The top came in March of 2001 when one of the companies involved in the boom, MicroStrategy, admitted to misstating its numbers to make its stock look better than it was. At the time MSTR was a multibillion-dollar $300-a-share company. The stock would quickly wilt to $3 a share. Suddenly, we began to worry: Was this all a mirage? Were we buying lottery tickets, as Greenspan suggested in a lucid moment? Were MicroStrategy and Ask Jeeves and Inktomi not the new blue chips? Were they just a bunch of frauds?

It was difficult to blame the young inexperienced team at MicroStrategy. They didn't want to let anyone down with

YOU GOT SCREWED! 59

disappointing numbers. And what was the penalty for creating better numbers than the company was capable of? *Nada.* Nil. Nothing. In the last couple of years one company after another—Waste Management, Cendant, and Sunbeam—had inflated numbers, and the SEC and the Justice Department seemed not to care. It seemed not a crime, but a benign form of exaggeration. What was the harm in that? The regulators didn't seem eager to prosecute under Clinton and government enforcers seemed defanged. Why not create rosy forecasts? And why not sell stock into them? What was the point of owning a stock if not to sell it into the hype when people wanted it?

Oh sure, a few investors took money off the table in 2000. But many people stayed fully invested unwilling to share the gains they had with the taxman. They thought it un-American to sell. Selling was for losers. Selling was for people who hadn't read *Stocks for the Long Run* and *Dow 36,000.* Selling was for people who didn't go on the Web and read The Motley Fool. Most people, instead of selling or buying bonds or diversifying, or just raising a little cash, simply watched and dutifully committed more money to the market, faithfully and without question. They rode everything, from dot-coms to established semiconductor and software companies, down from their highs without even blanching. Why not? Stocks are like parents, and owners are like kids lost at the mall, these investors told themselves. Parents always come back.

By the end of 2000, with the Naz cut 50% from its high, and tech stocks swooning daily, the Fed began cutting rates. That gave investors more impetus to stick around for Act II.

But it didn't matter. The areas where the people were

most heavily invested were the "blue-chip techs," which weren't dependent on higher or lower rates, just new tech cycles. But we were just plain out of cycles. The public didn't know that, though, as a generation of brokerage house strategists and mutual fund stalwarts preached that the only really great stocks were the ones with infinite growth, not the ones that paid dividends or grew only a little faster than the gross domestic product. Tech blue chips, with their unlimited growth and their prospects bound by no multiple, were the only safe place to be for the long term—a perversion of even the most bullish interpretations of the academics.

Frozen, the public watched things unravel. Nasdaq 5,000 melted into 4,000, then 3,000, 2,000, and finally, in a move that erased the whole gain since 1996, 1300. If you had gotten in during the early 1990s, you still had something to show for it, provided you sold! Everyone who came into the Nasdaq after 1997 pretty much lost everything.

The meltdown appeared at first to be restricted to the stocks that had been created during the booming but short-lived telecom heyday, when investors believed that the combination cellphone-television-camera-GameBoy-e-mail-bank-broker communicator was the way of the future. Then it spread to the Internet infrastructure stocks as people recognized that the Net, while important, wasn't nearly as transforming as the analysts and venture capitalists had said it was. The plague then hit the telecommunications providers, pole-axing Lucent and Nortel, as all of those start-up telcos ran out of money and began to default on their bonds and their loans to these providers. Then it traversed to the traditional tech stocks, Cisco and Intel, Sun and EMC, which had been thought to be immune because, heck, weren't they permanent-growth blue chips? No matter, they couldn't beat the earnings anymore, even after they brought down their projections to levels that they thought they could beat. Drats!

Then came the summer of 2001 and Enron, and later WorldCom, and soon the dominoes were falling. Then we realized that so much of what passed as "better than expected" earnings was invented for the simple reason that higher stock prices allowed executives to exercise their options and sell stocks at prices that the stocks never would have reached if everyone hadn't embraced the ridiculous "better than expected" standard. The joke was on us. The money stolen, trillions upon trillions of it, now sat in the hands of the very few who had been clever enough to rig the system.

Six

Executive Options

If you can come up with a surer plan for ripping out the lungs of the investor class than the current executive option compensation, my hat's off to you. The idea behind executive option compensation was to allow executives to become owners of their companies. Call it a reaction to the eighties, when the executives running the companies didn't own enough of the companies to matter. Their lack of ownership led to such abuses as large salaries and perks that made you feel these people were country club wards, not execs.

People forget that Gordon Gecko wasn't railing against managements that owned stock through options and sold it; he was railing against management that was paid extravagant cash salaries and owned *no* stock. Today, Gecko would be castigating the executives who granted themselves stock options, hyped their stocks, and then bailed. That's how far we went from an era when the execs had nothing at stake to one during which they lied to make their personal fortunes.

It would have been fine had we set up a system in which executives could buy stock slightly cheaper and then have to hold on to it. It is quite different to set up a scheme to reward executives with millions upon millions of options—not stock—that won't let them make money until they sell. We incentivized them to make short-term results by getting out quickly. It would be bad enough if that were all that was at stake, but we also allowed executives to write their own compensation packages. And because options didn't count against earnings—another accounting fiction—the more options the merrier. In other words, we created a compensation package wherein execs could make five, ten, fifteen, twenty, one hundred times more than the workers, and then we insisted that they sell the stock to realize those gains.

The result? The bizarre spectacle of executives who spend all of their time managing their stocks, not their companies. They got paid hundreds of millions of dollars to manage the Street's expectations so they could be beaten. Once the stock went higher, they could exercise calls and skedaddle. And, if the companies couldn't make the numbers that they set themselves, then the executives were allowed to reprice the options downward. *Even if the companies didn't do well,* the executives could still make a bundle.

Did the rank and file get to reprice? Are you kidding me? Of course not. Did you, the shareholder, get to reprice? Dream on.

So, a situation meant to put the executives on the same page as the suffering shareholders ends up giving them a much better position regardless of whether the business does well. It also rewards short-term stock performance over long-term corporate results; better to build a stock than to build a company.

This created the upside-down situation in which executives called analysts and told them to low-ball their earnings estimate. The compliant analysts did so, and the execs beat the "numbers." The dumbfounded media reported the "better than expected" numbers. Then when the stock flew, they exercised the options and sold while the mutual funds, ostensibly our stewards, bought more because the artificial matrix had been beaten. Was anyone not complicit in this giant executive-enrichment charade? And, of course, if the stock hadn't flown, they could have lowered the exercise price, exercised the options, and sold. Heads they win, tails you lose.

It's amazing to me that such a wrong-headed system could pass public muster, but these option plans pretty much defined the executive suite in the late 1990s and early 2000s, until, at last, Warren Buffett suggested that options actually count toward expenses, and Dick Grasso and the New York Stock Exchange demanded that listed companies submit these outrageous plans to a vote. Business captains initially blasted that proposal but later had to accept it because of public pressure. Still, the process of jamming boards of directors with cronies who would check off on anything is still the most prevalent pattern in business today. A board that is made up of outsiders is very rare even today.

When anyone complained about any part of this system, the executives mustered their considerable might, argued that rank-and-file workers would be hurt—even though only 10 percent of the nonexec workforce had any right to these options—and kept up the big-time scam.

Why didn't the shareholders revolt? Because the shareholders, for the most part, are mutual funds. They are just renting stocks and never gave a darn about corporate governance. They routinely "outsource" the review of corporate governance oversight to entities that don't have the manpower or the horse sense to spot even the most poorly disguised chicanery.

That means the mutual funds aren't paying any attention to executive options. These mutual funds are, in the end, just asset gatherers. Those of you who look at your proxies yourself and decide to vote against plans, good luck. Shareholders don't get to vote on most of the plans anyway, and you don't have the votes to stop anything egregious even if it were entered on the ballot. The mutual funds will just endorse it as a matter of course. It is a hapless and unrigorous process, a cross between a North Korean parliamentary exercise and local elections in Zimbabwe.

That's right—these public companies are run with benefits that private companies would only dream of having, with no real checks on them. Management can do what it wants. That's how Dennis Kozlowski from Tyco could loot millions upon millions of dollars from Tyco to buy houses, paintings, and a $6,000 shower curtain. It was how the Rigases could use Adelphia as their own piggy bank and nobody knew it. The notion of shareholder democracy is a total sham. The mutual funds didn't give a darn, because it wasn't their job to object to salaries and options packages when stocks were going higher.

The options game also makes executives do funny things when business goes bad. In Enron's case, the top execs hid the debt and obligations from the shareholders and the analysts so no one would know the liabilities. That propelled the stock ever higher so executives could pump up the stock with positive information and then blow out of the stock whenever it suited them. No questions asked.

Funny, but the worst abuser of the "beat the numbers" game was Qwest, the old U.S. West, run by Joe Nacchio. Qwest went to any lengths to make the numbers, including booking lots of business on Sundays at the end of quarters with companies that were barely in business. Qwest would send money to them as some sort of disguised payment for something, and the money would flow back in as earnings! This strategy worked well enough for so many quarters that Nacchio and his gang were able to sell hundreds of millions of dollars in stock into their incredibly sophisticated pump-and-dump operation.

Don't I know it. They tried to enlist me in their pump-and-dump schemes by telling me that they were in great shape when I was about to go on *Squawk Box* on CNBC. Fortunately, time ran out before I could let people know how fabulous they told me things were. And wasn't I lucky. The very next day Qwest announced that earnings would fall sharply below expectations. I wonder how many shares they would have sold had I had time to sing the company's praise.

Why did the executives think they could get away with this? Easy, because there had been multibillion-dollar frauds before, notably Waste Management, where accounting depreciation rules were violated systematically for years; Cendant's CU International division, where bogus revenues were a way of life; and Sunbeam, which cooked the books in so many different ways that the place resembled a school for accounting scandal.

In every single case no criminal prosecutions were brought against the top guns at these places. In fact, these companies gave CEOs a virtual chicanery road map that was followed en masse in 2000 when business went bad. None of these latter-day companies needed to try the shenanigans of that trio, so why not go for some fuzzy accounting? The reason so many lied is because so many got away with it before. The government had neither the will nor the inclination to prosecute white-collar fraud. It was too hard, and as long as stocks were going up, you couldn't find a jury that would convict anyway. So why waste your time?

Why weren't some of these moves caught by the professional auditors working for the companies? Sometimes the auditors were in on it. Other times the auditors regarded themselves as "partners" in the companies' efforts to beat the numbers. They were rewarded with big consulting contracts, provided they looked the other way.

Why didn't the government's auditors catch some of this stuff? Dream on—as we've said, the SEC is starved of money, part of a legacy of smaller government that both the Democrats and the Republicans checked off on. More auditors? More lawyers? That meant more money going to the SEC, and no one in Congress or the White House wanted that to happen.

Why didn't savvy shareholders see this stuff? Because the

accounting rules allow such latitude that even the worst of these crimes could somehow be considered generally accepted accounting principles.

Why didn't the so-called independent boards see this stuff? Because the directors' jobs were sinecures, and the desire to simply go to the meeting and pick up the check prevailed. Why not? You were covered by insurance if you screwed up anyway, and you didn't pay the premium. That's how we got the absurd situation in which audit committee members, the people who check the books—like Wendy Gramm, the former head of the Commodity Futures Trading Commission—could check off on options and futures schemes that were at best highly questionable, and at worst blatantly illegal, and then deny knowledge of the plans.

In other words, the pump-and-dump fix was in for most of the top executives of America. There weren't a few bad apples but whole orchards full of them. And there was no one standing in the way before the executives pumped their stocks, exercised calls, and dumped their stock. The media loved having on smiling execs who beat the numbers. Analysts, for reasons already discussed, were thrilled to talk up those companies that beat the numbers. And the government was so swamped it didn't even bother to check this stuff. In fact, the government, which routinely goes after little guys, including in one case a high school kid, for pumping and dumping on-line, hasn't brought a single case of pump and dump against one of these multihundred-million-dollar schemes.

Of course, for some the money and the options weren't good enough. They had to use their public companies as banks for big loans to be able to buy the CEO a house or to buy stock on margin when their stocks started coming down so they could wave the flag and show they believed! Why not? If the numbers were fudged, as at WorldCom, you wouldn't owe the money anyway and you could walk away from the loan. Gee, I wish some bank would offer me that deal.

It got so bad at the end of the era that Tyco executives wrote contracts that allowed their options to have "accelerated vesting" if they were fired—an eerie prelude. You have to be a veritable Lex Luthor to write that into your contract, but both the former CEO and the former general counsel of Tyco worked those clauses in, something we only found out after the stock plummeted and the CEO was indicted.

Egregious? Of course. Legal? Still. Amazing, isn't it? Amazing that after all we have been subjected to, the stock manager as CEO, with the lucrative options schemes drawn up at his own behest, still rules American business. It is the exception, the rarity, who *doesn't* play this game. Fortunately, as we shall find later, the exceptions can be found and they still can make you money, lots of it. But you have to know how to look for them and how to stay away from the business-as-usual types who have learned nothing from the biggest business scandals of all time.

Seven

Mutual Funds

Most people don't think of the mutual funds as villains in the great bear market that started in 2000. The mutual funds are viewed as innocuous asset-gatherers who, if anything, were victims of the shenanigans that separated so many from their money. As I like to say in my columns in TheStreet.com, *Wrong!*

Mutual funds are at the core of what is wrong with Wall Street, not what is right. They wield tremendous power by virtue of their commissions. They are able to move stocks up or down on a whim, particularly a whim that comes at the end of a quarter, when the funds are graded by the various newspapers and magazines that are slavishly devoted to rating funds by performance. By buying gobs of their own favorite stocks, their largest existing positions, at the end of every quarter, they are able to move the performance of these stocks upward by percentage points so the funds will get the acknowledgments that they need to take in more money. Fund managers typically have nothing at stake, aren't at risk with you—they may not even have money with their funds—and often have little or no training before they are given huge sums to manage.

Mutual funds played these games with your dollars end-lessly during the period when the television stations decided to give a free pass to anyone who shot out the lights. The in-cessant attention paid to "the hot hands" tilted the bias in favor of mutual funds buying the most aggressive compa-nies, the ones that could fly up the most. One appearance as a "hot hand" was worth thousands upon thousands of ad dollars, so why not go for the extreme! Some of the more egregious mutual funds virtually adopted stocks, bought huge gobs of them, and then "walked them up" as part of a weird circle wherein the more they bought, the higher their stocks went, the higher their stocks went, the more acco-lades the funds received, and therefore the more money that came in. The public, seeking the maximum performance and not understanding the risks if the market went south, poured billions into these kinds of funds. These all-offense mutual funds, which loved the riskiest stocks at all times, got the most praise from the media because the media relied on the percentage gains as the only litmus.

Television loved to put on the biggest gunners in the business, the mutual fund managers who bought the riskiest stocks that were making maximum rewards, who didn't even hint that perhaps, if things went bad, you could lose a fortune. Kevin Landis, manager of the First Hands family, became the most ubiquitous television mutual fund manager because of his mastery of the tech soundbite. He was not only responsible for hundreds of millions of lost dollars at the funds he managed, but billions more because of the glib way he presented techs as safe and prudent. They—and he—were anything but.

How many of these funds stressed their risky nature? Did they ever reveal what could happen with their go-go strategies if the market were to crack? Did they explain how they were dabbling in potentially dangerous, unseasoned stocks, or that they were, in some ways, just pyramid schemes, taking new money in to prop up the stocks that they already owned? Did the government bother to explain the risks to anyone even as the government turned everyone into portfolio managers handling 401k's and IRAs? Did anyone know how risky this whole enterprise was? No one from the mutual funds wanted you to know about this. They did everything they could to explain the rewards and hide the risks.

In fact, many funds hid behind their charters and claimed that they represented the aggressive portion of a person's portfolio when they knew they represented *all* of the person's portfolio. This built-in recklessness allowed these companies to justify enormous personal losses for peoples' nest eggs without an ounce of reflection, remorse, or apology. Heck, they still don't acknowledge they did anything wrong! It was always the market that went wrong, not them. No mutual fund has ever, to my knowledge, turned down someone for "suitability" reasons, meaning potential clients aren't appropriate for the fund's risk profile. So, people sent money to precisely the kind of aggressive growth funds they never should have invested in.

Who was running those funds? Often, people who knew nothing about stocks, other than how to pick the hottest ones out there. No licensing requirement, no test, nothing, precludes someone from running a mutual fund. The industry, during its peak, attracted pure gunners, those who were willing to take on any amount of risk to finish first in the percentage derby so they could gather assets. And why not? Unlike hedge funds, which are meant only for the wealthy, but place the manager alongside the client in the fund, these mutual funds were run strictly for a percentage of the assets under management. The goal was simply to raise as much money as possible, even though every academic study shows that once you have taken in more than several billion dollars you almost always cease to be anything other than an index fund. But the fees were so great that it was worth it to risk anything to get those assets under management.

These same managers came to believe that if they exercised any judgment—meaning if they built cash positions when they thought the market was too high or sold positions because the stocks had become too expensive—they weren't fulfilling their mandates. As the markets kept roaring, they kept throwing money into stocks regardless of the price, keeping cash as a minimum, *even though the people giving them money expected that some judgment would be exercised.*

Often, the large nature of their funds gave them an edge in performance. They were able to berate company management and find out things at companies that individuals couldn't because they could threaten to sell stock, causing the company's stock to plummet. Executives awash with options certainly didn't want that to happen. Fund managers were also able to find out things about companies from brokerage analysts that retail investors, without commission clout, could never do.

But in 2000, at the height of the bull market, the Securities and Exchange Commission put through Regulation Fair Disclosure, which forbade anyone, including the mutual funds, from finding out anything material from companies about their businesses, regardless of the ownership stake. Suddenly, the big research advantage of mutual funds vanished, and so did the funds' ability to "beat" the market. No longer could they barge in to chief financial officers of companies of which they owned 4 or 5% and say, "Tell us how you are doing or we will dump your stock with a fury." No longer could they berate chief executive officers into telling them things that no one else knew. And no longer could they "work" the analysts for information *before* the retail investors got wind of it. They lost the edge that came from their behind-the-scenes channels that they had cultivated in the late 1990s. They no longer knew what we didn't.

But did any of these funds say that they had lost their edge? Did any of them admit that Regulation FD took away whatever real appeal their big money, their scale, might have had? Nah, they continued to hold themselves out as diligent seekers of information, even though the special information that accrued to them because of their size vanished and they knew no more than anyone else.

No matter. Collectively, the mutual fund industry urged you to sit tight no matter what the costs or the risks or the lack of knowledge. These funds claimed to be diversified portfolio managers, but many were either just high-priced versions of S&P funds—for which they should have charged next to nothing in fees—or agglomerations of the hottest crap in the market. When the market cooled, they lost fortunes—your fortunes.

Of course, they kept mum about the bad news: that people began pulling money out in droves after a third straight year of losses. They lied rather than admit that they had to sell because of redemptions from the public. The mutual fund laws allow them to hide just about everything that you need to know about your money, from which stocks they own to how much cash they have and how much they have to send back to meet redemptions. So why not fib? Why bother to admit "Yep, we have money coming out and this is an unstable time." Consequently, you were at their mercy when they had to sell stocks at a loss to raise cash for people who finally got fed up with their losses and chose to redeem. This further weakened the price of the stocks that the funds urged you to hang on to.

One day the media will call everyone's attention to the mutual funds, but don't expect it soon. They are the largest advertisers in the financial media. To write what I just wrote in the pages of a financial magazine would be advertising suicide. The large mutual funds and the brokers who sell mutual funds would vanish, move their ads to another source, one that is less objective. Believe me, I have seen it with my own eyes. Janus Funds cancelled a $400,000 ad campaign with TheStreet.com when I casually mentioned in a column that I had told my dad to pull his pension money out of Janus because the firm was too concentrated in just a few names and wouldn't be able to get out of those companies when things turned bad.

The symbiotic nature of the mutual funds and the media should have been obvious. The monthly magazines needed to anoint new winners for their covers—the hottest managers sold better than those dowdy save-now-for-retirement covers. Television needed a steady diet of cheap talent to fill time, and mutual fund managers who loved stocks could fill that time better than anyone. And, if those same funds wanted to advertise on the networks, why not? Even the daily newspapers were hesitant to attack those who paid the bills. Better to focus elsewhere.

But if the truth were to come out, high on the list of America's most wanted bear profiteers would be the mutual funds, these great absentee minders of your hard-earned savings.

Eight

Brokerages

Investment banks hire research analysts to help sell deals that corporate finance brings in. There, that's the sum total of what you needed to know about those seemingly impartial experts that you heard from so often in the last few years. Until New York State Attorney General Eliot Spitzer released internal e-mails of Merrill Lynch to the world, most of the public really thought that analysts were out to try to help you make money in the market.

Many television personalities and their producers knew nothing about how the stock market worked anyway. Some actually thought that the analysts were experts, which they sure seemed to be when stocks were going higher. The television producers needed soundbites and live humans to appear on air and talk about stocks. Who cared if they weren't objective or if they were paid by some investment bank. And who wants to embarrass the guest on television by asking about potential conflicts. That wastes viewer time and could make people look corrupt—even if they were. Most of the time the reporters hadn't done enough homework to be skeptical and the producers didn't want to know about the conflicts. They just wanted the expert to play the role. It was totally shameless. Not until the stock market had already crumbled did television and print reporters start asking the tough questions about conflicts of interest. By then it was way too late to matter.

Of course, the experts turned out to be nothing more than housemen, the equivalent of movie critics paid by the studios. Why didn't we know this? Because fortunes were spent to keep you from knowing it. Most people genuinely believed that the analysts were paid by how they picked stocks. But other than at firms that did no investment banking, analysts were graded by how much business they helped bring in to corporate finance.

How did this all come about? Because the sales side, which used to generate large commissions and had lots of power internally at these firms, lost its clout with the slicing of commissions. The sales side still had lots of assets under management, but the people who made the most money at these firms were the investment bankers who sold and structured large deals to corporations, not stock buyers. These investment bankers called the shots. Research, on the other hand, generated no money on its own because no one pays for research on Wall Street. Research comes with the sales-peoples' phone calls: They tell you what to buy or sell and hope to get your order. Because of that disparity, the analysts' compensation came to be determined by corporate finance. Those who shilled the most and brought in the most deals were paid the most. That's how Jack Grubman became the highest-paid analyst on Wall Street. How can anyone be independent when the compensators are demanding that research be written to cultivate banking contacts? It was an impossible situation, and at many brokerage houses, even after all of the recent scrutiny, it still is.

Sometimes the conflicts were so egregious that the idea of objectivity, let alone service to the investor class, was absurd. Consider that Jack Grubman set himself up as a merger-and-acquisition specialist as well as a corporate finance salesman and researcher. Do you think the public knew that? Or do you think that the public thought that Grubman was working for it? If on the advice of Jack Grubman you bought and held Qwest, WorldCom, Global Crossing, Teligent, Winstar, Rhythms, or so many other smaller phone companies as they descended into oblivion, you probably thought Grubman was working for you. You didn't find out until it was too late to matter that he was working for them, and would downgrade them when every last stock and bond deal that could be done was done and there was no hope whatsoever of more business. That's how and when they came off the recommended list. Grubman was perhaps the nastiest example, but throughout the bull market into the dot-com bubble and beyond, analysts served simply as shills to help the bankers bring in deals.

What should really gall you about this is that everyone in the firms knew this. But they figured that as long as only the clever institutions and hedge funds realized that the brokers were running one giant promotional machine, they could continually gaff the public, which had been brainwashed into thinking that the only asset class that mattered was stocks. In other words, the sophisticated people, the hedge funds, guys like me when I ran Cramer Berkowitz, knew that Wall Street was a big racket, but as long as nobody said anything to the authorities and the authorities took campaign contributions from the lobbyists, so what? Until Eliot Spitzer, independent and wealthy, blew the whole thing wide open.

The brokers' research departments weren't the only bad actors, though. Many people succumbed to the easy credit that the brokers loaned to buy stocks on margin. Why not? They own the collateral and many individuals bought more and more stock on credit all the way down, only to find themselves wiped out when the bottom kept falling lower. Why did that happen? Once commissions had been cut so low, lending on stocks became the biggest profit center brokers had. The only way to make a good living selling stocks was to get people to borrow money to buy them.

Of course, not all brokers abetted the madness. But the electronic brokers, which included nary a human to speak to, encouraged people to buy stocks that were totally unsuitable for their risk profile and, worse, to ride them down to zero under the mistaken impression that stocks always come back.

At the height of the boom, all the brokers played on the theme of folks hitting it rich by playing the market in their spare time without any homework.

Should any of these brokers and analysts have seen the bust coming? Of course, they probably had more access to more negative information than just about anyone. But the word "sell" never entered into brokers' vocabularies until companies were so beleaguered or broke that no more financings could possibly be done for them. Only when the corpses were stone-cold did these analysts say, Sell.

What would have happened if the analysts had exercised judgment? The lesson of Enron was that if you said the emperor had no clothes, the company simply complained to its powerful friends in corporate finance and got you canned, then replaced by an analyst who was more compliant. This had been going on for years, but only after the devastation did the authorities step in. Until investment banking is separate from analysis not just in name but in reality, and the analysts are paid by how they perform in the market, this conflict will continue to taint the "profession," if you can call it that.

A few firms had it right and created real separation between the analysts and corporate finance to keep analysis independent, but the vast majority didn't, which is why their research can never be trusted again by any thinking person. Among the few good guys were Prudential, because they gave up on investment banking, and Morgan Stanley because the research bosses had power and integrity, the legacy of better days on Wall Street.

Part Three

Now What?

Nine

It's a Jungle Out There

So it's a jungle out there. We thought it might be a level playing field, with well-lit signposts and eager people willing to give us directions and a global positioning system to make money. Instead, it turned out to be triple canopied terror with poisonous snakes and Bengal tigers lurking behind every tree.

So what do we do? Do we stay at home, hide under the bed with our money between the box spring and the mattress? Do we accept the fact that our nest eggs are doomed to checking-account interest rates? Do we buy Canadian Maple Leaf gold coins and pray for the worst, knowing that the whole financial edifice from brokerage to mutual funds can't be trusted to do the right thing by us?

If your mattress paid rates that made retirement possible before age ninety, absolutely. If money were a potted plant, and we could just water it and give it some sun, well, then, investing would be easy.

But given the facts that we don't want to and can't work forever and that there are decent, honest alternatives available, we have to make our peace with the current environment. We have to find alternatives that work despite the forces that want to separate us from our money.

Fortunately, as someone who has seen every trick in the book that the complex of brokerage houses, mutual funds, media, and the academics have played on you, I know how to get you through the jungle unscathed. I don't have a magic machete, but I have been through the trails and I know the safest ways to go. I can get you to where you will be safe, but it certainly won't be as fun or as exciting as it was in the late 1990s. That was an aberrational period, and those investors waiting for it to come back will be doomed to disappointment.

First thing we have to do is break with the past. We have to stop believing that the market is going to roar back, as if it were some sort of spirited bull penned up in the Nasdaq center waiting for the chance to rampage back to 5,000. In fact, I think that the Nasdaq could be a poor performer for years, and that "tech blue chips" is strictly oxymoronic. We have to recognize that the vested interests all want us to believe that the Nasdaq is about to roar back. The biggest business brokers can do is restructuring business, but to do that they have to have enough suckers who will keep broken companies alive by thinking that they don't want to take the losses. Don't play that game. If you are in the Lucents, the Nortels, or the Qwests, admit defeat, sell, and move on. Those are broken companies that need to do a huge amount of investment banking to work their way out of their holes, if they ever will, and the common stock, the one you want to play with, will end up being worthless anyway. Stocks of companies that have been financed and refinanced and are still losing money aren't going to come back. They are better as losses taken than losses unrealized. Put the money you have left after you sell to productive use. You are wasting valuable time and capital that could be spent owning stocks that go up, stocks that pay dividends that compound with that capital appreciation.

If you can spend a couple of hours a week—not more than that—keeping track of the news and reading on the Web about your stocks, including their key filings, you will never be buried again. But if you can't do that, or you can't understand balance sheets, then you must seek the help of an investment adviser whom you trust, one that you get by referral. Ask your colleagues, your friends, your relatives, whoever in the financial industry did not let you down. You want an adviser who did not recommend a plethora of go-go stocks with crummy balance sheets or dot-coms with no earnings. Find someone who stuck by a philosophy that utilized bonds, higher-yielding stocks, and older, more seasoned companies, not someone who made his living hawking underwritings. Ask what his "book" of business is. If it was underwritings and newer stocks, then you are going to be poorly served. But if he is a generalist who mixed investments and favored diversification in an attempt to build an ideal portfolio that was bulletproof to the collapse in the Nasdaq you might have your man—or woman. You have to find someone who understands the risks and the rewards of equities and who can help you find out whether companies you are looking at are solvent or not. You don't necessarily need a certified financial analyst helping you, just someone who can help interpret your risk profile and your goals into a suitable portfolio. Be sure the person was never written up for a violation of the New York Stock Exchange rules and make sure to ask for referrals. When I worked at Goldman Sachs, I always had a list of people I worked with who were happy with my performance. If someone won't give you a couple of referrals, avoid that person. Make sure the adviser likes homework and doesn't think it is something that should be shirked or outsourced to the "research department." You don't want someone who can be an escort to parties and you don't want someone who can get you courtside tickets. Heck, you don't even want someone who will pal around with you. You just need someone whom you can talk to for help in building and monitoring a portfolio.

Let's banish "buy and hold" for good. Remember that what matters is doing homework before, during, and after you have purchased a stock. You must be sure the company underneath isn't too expensive and can pay its dividend or increase it in time. That's how we will make the big money going forward. "Buy and hold" is a bogus philosophy invented as a way to take your eye off the ball. Every financial planner, mutual fund expert, and broker hid behind buy and hold as you lost money. Every one of these charlatans neglected to tell you that buying and holding bad stocks was dumb as a bag of hammers. The term you should remember is "buy and homework," not buy and hold.

How imperative is it that you be able to read a balance sheet? Only in so far as you understand that some companies owe a lot of money in debt and may not be able to pay it. To the extent that you can read even that much, you will do fine. Why do you need to know that? Because the companies that got in huge trouble in this era, as in all eras, did so not because their stocks were overvalued but because they took down too much debt, either in the form of bank debt or public debt, such as senior or junior bonds. All of that debt mattered because when the companies went belly-up the common stock that people owned, and often continued to buy for dimes and quarters, was worthless. The folks holding the senior securities wound up owning the common stock in the new enterprise. Every other security got warrants to own the new enterprise except the holders of common stock, which was worthless, even though the cynical exchanges continued to let the worthless stock trade to make small fees on each transaction. It is not that hard to distinguish a clean balance sheet, where the common stock is unthreatened, from a dirty one, where the common stock is in the danger zone. Take a look at these two balance sheets, Philadelphia Suburban and Tyco. The first is clean, just like the water it provides, and has ample room for the company to raise its dividend—which it keeps doing—and to buy back stock. The second is a basket case. Even as its stock crashed from $60 to $10, Tyco couldn't buy back any stock and couldn't raise its dividend because of its overwhelming interest charges. It had to repay loans that it had borrowed to make reckless acquisitions.

Ahh, but would balance-sheet sleuthing have kept you from buying a dot-com with no debt or a new technology company with no earnings? No, which is why we need to have other criteria, criteria that have worked for me in all kinds of markets in the last three decades.

TYCO INTERNATIONAL LTD

	JUNE 30, 2002	SEPTEMBER 30, 2001
Current Assets:		
Cash and cash equivalents.................................	$ 2,793.9	$ 1,779.2
Accounts receivables, less allowance for doubtful accounts ($575.1 at June 30, 2002 and $550.4 at September 30, 2001)...	6,604.5	6,453.2
Inventories (Note 12)....................................	5,242.6	5,101.3
Deferred income taxes....................................	763.1	980.2
Other current assets (Note 12)..........................	1,460.1	1,532.3
Total current assets..................................	16,864.2	15,846.2
Net Assets of Discontinued Operations.....................	4,387.9	10,598.0
Construction in Progress -- Tyco Global Network............	743.6	1,643.8
Tyco Global Network Placed in Service, Net.................	202.9	698.6
Property, Plant and Equipment, Net (Note 12)..............	10,480.3	9,970.3
Goodwill, Net...	27,077.0	23,264.0
Intangible Assets, Net....................................	6,522.1	5,476.9
Other Assets (Note 12)...................................	4,321.5	3,524.8
TOTAL ASSETS..	$70,599.5	$71,022.6
Current Liabilities:		
Loans payable and current maturities of long-term debt....	$ 5,411.3	$ 2,023.0
Accounts payable...	3,268.6	3,692.6
Accrued expenses and other current liabilities (Note 12)...	5,544.7	5,181.8
Contracts in process -- billings in excess of cost........	535.5	935.0
Deferred revenue...	733.2	973.5
Income taxes payable.....................................	2,003.0	1,845.0
Total current liabilities.............................	17,496.3	14,650.9
Long-Term Debt..	20,715.8	19,596.0
Other Long-Term Liabilities (Note 12).....................	5,129.5	4,736.9
TOTAL LIABILITIES...................................	43,341.6	38,983.8
Minority Interest...	55.6	301.4
Shareholders' Equity:		
Preference shares, $1 par value, 125,000,000 shares authorized, one share outstanding at June 30, 2002 and September 30, 2001 (Note 6)..........................	--	--
Common shares, $0.20 par value, 2,500,000,000 shares authorized; 1,995,423,531 and 1,935,464,840 shares outstanding, net of 26,151,932 and 17,026,256 shares owned by subsidiaries at June 30, 2002 and September 30, 2001, respectively (Note 6)...........................	399.1	387.1
Capital in excess:		
Share premium..	8,146.4	7,962.8
Contributed surplus, net of deferred compensation of $92.6 at June 30, 2002 and $85.3 at September 30, 2001..	14,762.3	12,561.3
Accumulated earnings.....................................	4,944.3	12,305.7
Accumulated other comprehensive loss.....................	(1,049.8)	(1,479.5)
TOTAL SHAREHOLDERS' EQUITY...........................	27,202.3	31,737.4
TOTAL LIABILITIES AND SHAREHOLDERS' EQUITY...........	$70,599.5	$71,022.6

Note: All figures in millions

PHILADELPHIA SUBURBAN CORP

	June 30, 2002	December 31, 2001
Assets	(Unaudited)	
Property, plant and equipment, at cost	$ 1,754,001	$ 1,677,061
Less accumulated depreciation	327,087	308,946
Net property, plant and equipment	1,426,914	1,368,115
Current assets:		
Cash and cash equivalents	876	1,010
Accounts receivable and unbilled revenues, net	53,222	56,331
Inventory, materials and supplies	4,819	4,446
Prepayments and other current assets	5,120	8,085
Total current assets	64,037	69,872
Regulatory assets	79,458	79,669
Deferred charges and other assets, net	20,023	22,915
Funds restricted for construction activity	30,132	19,768
	$ 1,620,564	$ 1,560,339
Liabilities and Stockholders' Equity		
Stockholders' equity:		
6.05% Series B cumulative preferred stock	$ 816	$ 1,116
Common stock at $.50 par value, authorized 100,000,000 shares, issued 69,755,662 and 69,300,346 in 2002 and 2001	34,878	34,650
Capital in excess of par value	311,191	304,039
Retained earnings	158,212	149,682
Minority interest	527	787
Treasury stock, 963,986 and 913,877 shares in 2002 and 2001	(18,356)	(17,167)
Accumulated other comprehensive income	378	726
Total stockholders' equity	487,646	473,833
Long-term debt, excluding current portion	573,487	516,520
Commitments	-	-
Current liabilities:		
Current portion of long-term debt	13,849	14,935
Loans payable	97,736	109,668
Accounts payable	15,200	27,667
Accrued interest	8,505	8,302
Accrued taxes	19,833	22,865
Other accrued liabilities	19,553	19,198
Total current liabilities	174,676	202,635
Deferred credits and other liabilities:		
Deferred income taxes and investment tax credits	170,407	167,577
Customers' advances for construction	67,407	59,886
Other	10,960	9,204
Total deferred credits and other liabilities	248,774	236,667
Contributions in aid of construction	135,981	130,684
	$ 1,620,564	$ 1,560,339

What are the benchmarks that we need to buy the good and stay away from the bad? Let's review them. Everything you need is accessible via the Web and all this information can be spotted with the same ease and similar amount of homework that would have gotten you a B on a tenth-grade paper, or allowed you to finish in the middle of your office football or March Madness pool.

Dividends

First, we are going to have to go back to the quaint days when we inquired about a company's dividend. As interest rates could remain low in a low-growth, low-inflation economy, we aren't going to be able to pick up as much interest in our cash or our fixed-income investments. Right now there are lots of companies that yield much more than cash, much more than ten- or thirty-year bonds, with much more upside and, frankly, not as much downside if the economy heats up. (Bonds go down in price and up in interest if the economy begins to grow at a faster pace.)

How do we find these good dividend-paying stocks? First, what's a hefty dividend that gives us "yield protection," meaning something that offers a return on the dividend alone that is better than you would get from the bank? To me, a yield of 3% or greater is a terrific start, offering a percent-and-a-quarter more return than you would get in cash at present, and of course, a lot more upside! If the stock gets hit further and you like the company—in other words, if the stock price is damaged but not the company's sales or earnings—you will be able to buy the stock at a cheaper price. And you will earn a higher yield as yields go up when stock prices go down because yield is simply the amount of the dividend over the price of the common stock. Yield is just the dividend stated in percentage or fraction form. Stocks such as Bank of America, Royal Dutch/Shell, Philip Morris, ChevronTexaco, Fleet Boston, and DuPont all make sense as dividend plays, where I think you can buy with a degree of confidence that you will be protected in rough seas. So, let's say you buy Bank of America at $68. It has a $2.40-per-year dividend and therefore yields 3.5%. If the stock drops to $58, the dividend amount stays constant, but it now yields 4.1% and will attract other buyers. This also entices you to buy more, something that you don't feel particularly good about when you buy stocks with no dividend that have gone down. That's yield protection.

Why are dividends such a great indicator of corporate performance? Because companies don't issue dividends lightly. They weigh the matter and make a determination that the company's business is on track for the long term. It is embarrassing to issue a dividend and then cut it; there is shame involved and damage to the company's reputation. Dividends represent the gold standard of what a company aspires to, and they require, in many cases, years of good management and growth before a company can declare them. They are the only real signs of wealth and corporate progress.

Companies that don't have dividends or pay meager dividends may not have the performance and the history that you need to invest with confidence. I know most tech companies don't pay dividends, but rather than excusing them for that, I think you should question whether they are right for you. When Jeremy Siegel wrote *Stocks for the Long Run,* among the key components that led to his conclusion that stocks outperform all asset classes is the payment and then subsequent reinvestment of dividends. The compounding power of the dividends makes all the difference, and our recent loss of interest in dividends cost all of us dearly.

Insider and Corporate Buying

It is not enough just to buy stocks that have good dividends. You need outward signs that things are well. Look for these two clues: insider buying and corporate buying. Insider buying is available for free on the Web simply by hitting up the ticker symbol on a bunch of Web sites, including TheStreet.com, MarketWatch, and Nasdaq.com.

Why should we care about insider buying? Because people sell stocks for millions of reasons, everything from taxes to estate planning, buying homes, paying college tuitions. People buy stocks only for one reason: to make money. Sure, there will be occasional wrong-headed buys from some stubborn managements, but for the most part insiders who buy in a pattern are worth betting with, not against. This method has always been a handy way to beat the market in thick and thin. As someone who has watched insider buying all my trading life and handled quite a few insider buying orders, I value this methodology above almost all others. I love it when I see open-market buying of my stocks by executives, and I like to join them when they do it.

Companies that think their stocks are too cheap and that have excess cash after their expenses and dividends typically like to announce buybacks to sop up supply and to keep up the price of their stock. To find corporate buying you have to check recent business news reports, also available on the Web, to see if buybacks are in place.

How do these work? Each day, except for a few days before and after a quarter is announced, the company's treasurer places an actual order with either a broker or directly with the New York Stock Exchange floor broker if the company is listed on the NYSE. Such an order supports a stock, cushioning it from the vicissitudes of a volatile market. Some of the larger and more important buybacks of substance include those at Merck, Pepsi, and, again, Philip Morris. Not all companies that announce buybacks exercise them; some are just phantom. Make sure you look at the number of shares that are "taken out" or "crunched" by a buyback. If it is nothing, you know that the announcement was done for show. You can call the investor relations person at the company or check the quarterly filings to avoid phantom buybacks. You are looking to see whether the share count—the number of shares outstanding—has actually shrunk, or whether the buyback was just an illusory statement of support.

Not all buybacks are intelligent uses of capital. Many tech companies have been buying back stock for two years, and it has meant next to nothing for shareholders. In fact, most of these tech companies would do better to issue the dividends directly to shareholders instead of buying back stock. That's because the stocks are *expensive*. Sometimes the buybacks for tech companies are just a way to rein in all of the options these companies shower on their executives. If they issue 10 million shares in options, they buy back 10 million shares in the open market. That's not a buyback designed to shrink the outstanding stock, which is what you want to see; that's just enough to keep the shares running in place! In some cases companies borrow money to buy back stock because the interest on the borrowings is deductible but dividend payments aren't deductible. But if companies hit tough patches, they can cancel the dividends. They can't cancel the debt they borrowed to buy the stock, so instead, the common stock is wiped out if the company declares bankruptcy. That's why a lack of debt, or at least a manageable amount of debt on the balance sheet, which doesn't overwhelm the amount of money a company takes in, is so important. For stocks to work for you over the long term, you can't run the risk that the companies of your stocks will declare bankruptcy and destroy the common stock.

Fair Value

We don't want companies that are inherently overvalued, either, as again, they are more dangerous because they can fall faster and harder than inexpensive companies. They are more risky over the long term. Remember how mutual funds overlooked valuation and lost fortunes? Remember how brokerage house analysts developed new matrices because they couldn't justify owning stocks using traditional price-to-earnings multiples? Remember how the cable companies told us to look at their earnings before income taxes, depreciation, and amortization?

Well, now remember this, those recommendations were wrong, and they are nest-egg wreckers. The beat-the-street-by-a-penny crowd is a moronic one, and we don't want to be enticed into doing what they are doing. They are Circes trying to lure us from our money. So is the crowd that urges us to find new and unconventional ways of valuing stocks. So is the crowd that urges us to speculate on low-dollar turnarounds or penny stocks that have no earnings. We have a method of valuing companies and it has rarely if ever failed us for longer than a few years at a time: price-to-earnings multiples. Here's a good rule of thumb to remember: don't buy stocks with high price-to-earnings multiples even if they are growing fast, because they are too risky. You can own one or two of these stocks in a portfolio of say, ten stocks—more on portfolio size later—but you shouldn't own stocks that are too risky, and one of the most important risk variables is price.

This makes sense, as most of investing does, until Wall Street throws in its gibberish to spin your head and take your eye off the ball. In real life when you buy something expensive that isn't of high quality, you get ripped off. Same with the stock market. Sure, there will be periods when you are going to miss some opportunity, which is why I am willing to allow you to own a couple of stocks that have high price-to-earnings ratios, but in the 1990s we stopped even caring about this key measure. We must never let that happen again, and believe me, it can. It will because it is too convenient for all of those who want to unload their wares on you and don't want you to recognize the risks.

Why do I bother to stress the significance of the uniform way to value stocks? How about a concrete example. All my trading life the cable companies begged to be valued at a multiple to their earnings before income taxes, depreciation, and amortization (EBITDA) because they told us they had a very heavy upfront cost that would be paid back for years. They assured us that these costs would be paid with payments from lifetime cable subscribers as part of the companies' legal monopolies. But, at the same time, a new technology, the satellite dish, came along and started stealing cable customers at rates that made all of the suppositions wrong and destroyed values overnight. We never got the big earnings, and we therefore never got the big buybacks, dividends, or protection that we needed. Stockholders and fortunes were lost. In the wacky 1990s, we settled on a host of methodologies to value stocks that had no earnings, such as the multiple to EBITDA. Similarly, some analysts tried to get us to value companies by price-to-sales because they had no earnings. If they have no earnings, don't buy them.

Sure, you are liable to miss some big companies, but the home runs, the Home Depots and the Microsofts, where 100 shares from 1982 and 1986, respectively, made you millions, were profitable from the earliest days they came public, so the earnings requirement won't eliminate many great companies.

Understand, prudence is going to cut off our upside. But as a money manager who compounded at 24% after all fees for fourteen years, I can tell you that I willingly cut off the upside potential to minimize my downside. I do the same now with my personal portfolio, which is available on the Web via subscription at ActionAlertsPlus.com. I don't like to swing for the fences; I like to get on base and let the power of the dividends and earnings growth work for me over time. Think about how much more money you would have right now if your mutual fund manager had thought about such things. I like to be cautious. I want to make my money over time, not today, because if I make it all today, I can just as easily lose it all tomorrow.

How can we be sure that, after all our homework, we don't fall prey anyway to a Tyco or an Enron or a WorldCom or a Rhythms? Here are some simple steps to avoid those situations that are rife with conflict and risk.

First, we need to know about the governance of the company. The boards of directors of poorly performing stocks tend to be ones with big boards filled with insiders and cronies. The good boards have no insiders on them beyond the chief executive officer. Take a look at the boards of two fine companies known for their governance, Fortune Brands and American Standard. Both have made a point of telling me that they would never have any insiders grading them because they would be graded too lightly. Look at the proxy statement. Does it have lots of executives from within the company on the board? That's a loser plain and simple with rare exceptions that you won't recognize unless you are a pro.

We don't want imperial CEOs who give themselves outrageous pay packages. You can find out about this by looking at the proxy statements that come out once a year. We don't want to see our CEOs in *Vanity Fair* or *People* magazine. We want them in their offices, in the field, meeting with clients. We don't want poster boys, we want wonks who think that business is hard and tough and requires massive devotion to one's knitting, not to the press or other execs. We don't want the Bob Pittmans, ex of AOL, the Jean-Marie Messiers, ex of Vivendi, or the Thomas Mid-

delhoffs, ex of Bertelsmann, all of whom were more comfortable in the society pages then they were in the business
pages. We also don't want young whippersnapper chief financial officers. I don't mean to denigrate youth, but please
remember that those CFOs who have never been through
the mill and don't have years of experience may be the first
to panic and do something untoward. Glamorous CEOs
who manage the stock and the press and not their companies should be avoided at all costs.

How about the corporate books? What makes one company's more honest than another's? First, we don't want to
see multiple charges to earnings. That often masks what's
really going on because the managers can add back the
charges later to smooth earnings and cover up a deteriorat-
ing business. These reserves, or honeypots, as they are
called, were how Sunbeam hid its fraud so effectively. Lots
of charges are a sure sign that management is hiding things.
Avoid these companies. Big charges have become so common at IBM that I don't want to own that stock. They became a regular course of business at Tyco before that stock
came unglued. They are often a sign that management has
lost control of its business but wants to make you think that
it is only a one-time thing when it is a constant. Charges are
easy to spot. Instead of giving you the simple earnings in
generally accepted accounting terms, a company will give
you pro forma earnings or what earnings would have looked
like if all were well. Of course, you would never tell the
bank, if you were applying for a mortgage, here are my financials as they would be had I gotten a raise or had I in-
herited the money as I expected. Companies do that kind of
stuff all of the time, and we don't want to own the stocks of

companies that are trying to say, "Here's how we believe we look as opposed to the raw numbers that paint an ugly picture." That ugly picture is the real deal, and that's what you will own once you have bought stock in the company.

We don't want companies that are serial acquirers, companies that have made their business every few quarters by buying other companies. Sure, there are synergies that can be taken out, but buying companies may mean that the organic growth of the business doesn't exist. Serial buying is a terrific way to hide the true fundamentals of a company. Is this methodology going to keep you out of some good stocks? Of course, but it only takes one Tyco to wipe out years' worth of winners, and we can't asterisk your funds with a note that says, "We would have done even better if we hadn't bought this one particular loser."

We want simple financials, not complicated ones. Did your company hire a banker to move debt off balance sheets or create special-purpose entities? Many companies such as J. P. Morgan Chase and Citigroup specialized in dressing up financials—putting lipstick on pigs, as we say. They created shells that allowed companies like Enron to unload debt into the shells to hide it from both the ratings agencies like Standard & Poor and Moody's as well as unsuspecting potential investors. We are going to have to say no to companies like that. That's the price that Enron made other companies pay. If the financials can't be understood in a couple of pages, the business may simply be too complicated and too difficult to understand, or it may be that the company is hiding something. The federal government, despite all of the handwringing, still allows this kind of hide-the-debt maneuvering and until the government stops it, we have to watch for companies that footnote special-purpose entities to hide debt and make companies look less indebted than they are. Fortunately, there are on-line services that tell you about this stuff, that red-flag it for you. My favorite is The Turnaround Report by Arne Alsin, a professional money manager who specializes in forensic accounting and who has kept me out of trouble in situations where the debt wasn't obvious. (The Turnaround Report is available at TheStreet.com.)

We don't want to see two classes of stock in any situation. We favor one man, one vote, just like the Constitution of the United States, none of this one man, ten votes, if that man is in the founding family, and one man one vote if not. Many of the cable and newspaper companies are set up that way to preserve the rights of the original owners. This is a travesty because it allows the original owners to abuse the rest of us. I don't care how terrific the owners are; we don't want to be at their mercy because they have more votes. One man, one vote, must be the rule.

We also don't want to be in tracking stocks, pieces of paper meant to bring out value within a company because they track different operating divisions that aren't truly separate companies. These are just devices to raise money at your expense. These are too easily crammed down—just ask the holders of MCI or Rainbow Media. When WorldCom was struggling, it issued a tracking stock for its long-distance business that looked to have a very big dividend. But a year later WorldCom canceled the dividend and crushed the stock. Cablevision, the New York–based cable company, did the same thing with Rainbow Media. It told you that it was going to issue shares in an entity that represented a call on

YOU GOT SCREWED! 105

the interests of some of the company's most valuable prop-
erties. But when times got tough for the parent, it bought
back the tracking stock for a fraction of the price at which
it had been issued two years before. It took fortunes out of
the hands of investors and got away with it. In addition, we
never ever want to own stocks subsidiary to a parent when
the parent can erase the rights of the subsidiary, no matter
how attractive the situation might be.

Consider the case of AT&T Wireless, a spin out of
AT&T. Here was a company that AT&T still controlled after it spun it out. AT&T mercilessly dumped the rest of its
stock on the market, driving the stock into oblivion. It was
a costly lesson that you don't want to own stocks spun off of
entities when the entities remain in control of the rest of
the stock. AT&T Wireless was cut from $30 to $10 in no
time. It later went to the single digits when it was clear that
the predictions AT&T made about the business's growth
couldn't be met.

Given the premium that we must put on management
and the *seasoning* of management, we don't want to own
companies that are headed by someone who hasn't been a
CEO for a couple of years. And we don't want someone
who is in his first or last year of being a CEO. Breaking in is
too hard, succession too difficult. The first year for a CEO
at great companies like Home Depot, General Electric, and
Best Buy were all brutal. Take heed, you don't want the
pain! Companies make a big deal about a new CEO; there
are always lots of articles about the succession. When you
see these, vamoose, because the new CEO will screw it up
or make low-ball projections that he knows he can meet but
which will also immediately drive down the stock price. If

you don't know how long a CEO has been in, simply call the investor relations office of the company and they will tell you.

What should your portfolio look like after you have placed all of these limits on it? Let's get back to the notion that there are two components of a portfolio that are not trash: bonds and cash. Both can play a role. If you are, for example, investing for retirement, depending on your age, you may not have a lot of years to let stocks compound for you. People in their twenties and thirties need to be in stocks, as they can recover from any reversals that the stock market might experience in the time between when they started investing and when they retire. Younger people also have lots of income years ahead of them to be able to reinvest. People who bought stock in the 1970s, one of the worst decades for investing, and then continued to invest for the next twenty years, made millions in the market. They had to stay in and continue to contribute, though, to get the full effect of the compounding of growth and dividends. As you get closer to retirement, owning some bonds makes sense because you may not be able to make up stock losses in the time you have left to work and earn income. In your forties, for example, convertible bonds make sense as a way to enjoy both growth and capital preservation. These bonds give you yield protection but also allow you to participate if the common stock moves up big. The best way to be involved with converts, though, is not to own them individually, but to be in a convertible bond fund, such as the ones offered by Vanguard or Fidelity.

In your fifties I think a mixture of corporate bonds and treasuries makes sense for almost half of your portfolio, unless you have no plans to retire until you are in your seventies or eighties. Then you can still have a preponderance of common stock because you will have time to make up for any reversals that may occur in the market.

Keep some cash on hand each year and don't invest all at one gulp. Almost every year there has been a moment, a disastrous moment, when buying stock then could have made sense. Be ready. You would be surprised how few people ever seem to have any cash on hand. Why? Because they like to buy all at once; they want to call the bottom or make a statement.

My best investing times have come in any given year when I have been able to pounce on that period when stocks had fallen 20% from their peak. It happened even in the good years in the middle of the nineties. So I budgeted for it by keeping cash in my accounts.

In all my great years of investing I never did things all at once; I did them in stages. I invested over time. If I wanted a thousand shares of Philip Morris, I didn't go out and buy a thousand shares. I bought a couple of hundred shares and then waited. If the stock went up big right after, sometimes I sold, but invariably, the stock went down and I was able to buy at better prices. It is hubris and a lack of recognition of the fallibility of both man and markets that people plunk down their money all at once. If I am afraid to do it, you should be, too. Don't play the role of the big man who knows that this level or that price is the lowest a stock will trade. Accept that we are human and we often move too early or too late, and adjust for that in your thinking.

I don't care which stocks you buy, just don't buy too many of them. Imagine that your whole portfolio can be put on one piece of paper in one safe place. That's ideal. If you own twenty stocks, you might as well be a mutual fund. But if you own too few stocks you can't get the power of diversification working for you. Own liquid stocks and liquid investments that can be found easily in the *Wall Street Journal*. Don't confuse your heirs by owning something that can't be understood. After you are gone it will be sold for nothing, believe me.

Above all, remember that diversification is your only friend in the business. If you have the ability to buy and monitor a portfolio of stocks, you must be sure that they are from different groups and not concentrated in one area. I think that you need a minimum of five stocks to develop a diversified portfolio. Fewer than that and you haven't spread the risk effectively. How important is diversification? Put it this way: I have been doing a national radio show, *Jim Cramer's RealMoney,* and every Wednesday I play "Am I Diversified," where callers name me their top five holdings. When I started, people would call me and ask, "Jim, I own Dell, Microsoft, Intel, Micron, and Gateway—am I diversified?" I would have to explain that those stocks all track each other. You might as well own one stock! The goal is to be in a bunch of different industries so you can be immune from a downturn that affects one industry, whether it is pharmaceuticals, casinos, defense stocks, or, as was the case through much of America, technology stocks. Don't let things overlap. Would you order a steak, a hamburger, and a pork chop for dinner? It's the same in stocks.

There are so many habits to be broken when it comes to individual stocks, but the first is that it is okay to sell. If a company's business goes bad, it is okay to sell. If the company's management changes and you don't like the new folks, it is okay to sell. I believe that stocks that are damaged by the market are opportunities, but stocks of companies that are damaged themselves are dangerous. Consider the case of Wal-Mart versus Kmart. Many times in the last few years Wal-Mart's stock has been clocked because it is a big member of the S&P 500 and it went down when for some reason the S&P 500 dropped. Kmart did, too. But when stocks rallied, Wal-Mart participated, but Kmart didn't, because Wal-Mart's stock was damaged by the market, but Kmart's stock was simply damaged goods.

If a stock goes up hugely, it is imperative that you sell at least some. As my wife, the Trading Goddess, always said to me during our years trading together, "Bulls make money, bears make money, and pigs get slaughtered!"

If you take some money off the table as a stock goes up, you end up playing with the house's money. Then if there is a sudden downturn, you won't be screwed. Imagine if you had done this with your Sun or your EMC or your Cisco or your Microsoft! Selling is a necessary and vital tool in the arsenal of investing. Learn to do it and get comfortable with it.

Remember at all times, you have to sell the losers. People like to hold on to their losers and sell winners. I like to sell pieces of my winners on the way up. It is not a bad idea to see if you can do some trimming every ten points up, as you can always buy it back. I like playing with the house's money, the profits from a sale. However, if I own some stocks of damaged companies, that's a different story. That's where that buy-and-homework stuff comes in. You have to know whether a company's fortunes are fading. The market can pull down the stocks of good companies, and that's when you buy them. The fundamentals can pull down the companies themselves; that's when you sell them.

Where do you find this information if you can't see it? How about TheStreet.com, where we spend more time red-flagging stocks than anyone else. Spotting and eliminating dogs is huge, a large part of investing. You can't pretend they don't exist and you can't ride them down to zero. I can send you to other places for this information, but I set up TheStreet.com so you would be able to find this information quickly and completely. Don't consider it a warranty, just a sort of house or car inspection that you would normally do before making such a big-ticket purchase.

Never borrow money to be in the market. Ever. Borrowing money is for the pros, not the amateurs, and even the pros shouldn't do it except on very special occasions. Stocks are pieces of paper, and they aren't meant for borrowing against. Stocks aren't homes; they can go down in value much faster than your home can, and they can be reclaimed so fast by your broker that you won't even know what happened to your money. As a professional investor, I only borrowed money a very few times, and every time it was riskier than I liked. It can take you out of the game if the market goes south, and any investor knows the market goes south quite regularly. And when you least expect it.

In fact, let's go a step further. If your broker entices you to use margin, or talks about the ease of borrowing, fire him. More than $250 billion in margin loans were let out at the top of the market in 2000—the most money borrowed to buy stock in history—and almost everyone who borrowed got wiped out. Why don't you read more about this? Because, as someone who has done foreclosures on peoples' stocks, I can tell you it isn't a very public matter. It is every bit as sad and pathetic as when someone repossesses a house, though.

If you choose stocks wisely and buy wisely and not in big gulps, borrowing should never be a problem. You should always have enough cash on hand to buy more if you need to, and you should be ready to buy more. One of the worst things that happened to people at the turn of the millennium was that they bought stocks they did not understand, companies that made products they did not understand. When the stocks went down, they panicked and sold instead of buying more.

The professionals love it when their stocks "come in" for sale because they can buy more at discounted prices. The amateurs freak out. When a department store throws a sale for your favorite merchandise, do you freak out, or do you save up and buy? You should approach the stock market with the same kind of attitude. Unfortunately, most times people buy because of tips. If you own Lucent or Nortel, ask yourself whether you even know what they make. Do you know what Komag or Brocade makes? Do you know what Novellus or AMAT makes? If you don't, then why do you own these stocks? But, if you had bought stocks with good dividends that made products you understand, when the stock price dropped, would that have enticed you to buy more rather than caused you to kick it out?

If you don't have time to pick individual stocks or you don't or can't do any homework, there are alternatives, of course, but the alternatives require work, too. There is no situation I can even contemplate where you don't monitor your finances. But let's say you decide that you don't have that hour or two a week to spend on the homework. You can give your money to a mutual fund. But let's speak candidly about that industry, which is *never* spoken about candidly.

There is an arrogance to the mutual fund industry that is in part unintentional. When you speak to the customer representatives, you are speaking to the lowest people on the financial totem pole. They know nothing about the funds they are pushing, neither the risks nor the rewards nor even the names of the managers, and they aren't supposed to. They are told to exercise no judgment. Yet people keep coming to them because they are the only people you are allowed to speak to.

This situation, of course, is ridiculous because it is your money. But it gets worse. These funds also instruct their customer representatives not to give out the holdings of the funds or tell the clients what the disposition or outlook of the managers is. That's relegated to canned interviews with people from in-house reporting staffs a couple of times a year. If you think this sounds like the old Kremlin, you are right, it does. The whole nature of this industry baffles me. Here's why. When rich people gave their money to me to manage for them, they were entitled to know everything about me, my family, my views, and my favorite stocks. They knew my work hours, the names of my assistants, my likes and my dislikes. They knew my top-ten holdings and how I felt toward them at any given time. They were free to ask me any questions. Why? *Because it was their money.*

Of course, the mutual funds would tell you that they manage so many peoples' money that they can't possibly provide that level of detail. That's nonsense. They deliberately obfuscate and tell you nothing because they don't want you to know anything. They could post their holdings and their views on the Web, they could be transparent, but that would be asking for too much from them because *they don't think it is your money.* Some firms post a top-ten holdings list but it is almost always kept deliberately out of date. And funds have to report their holdings only every six months. What nonsense! I had to tell the rich people in my fund what they owned any day they asked. So should the mutual funds! Why is it that the rich are the only ones afforded this privilege of knowing how their money is managed? Mutual funds act as though it is their money. They exercise almost no judgment for you and they act as if they are doing a great deal for you.

Of course, there are some fund managers who make exceptions. But no manager I know is willing to do what a hedge fund manager does when he is running too much money—send the money back. No mutual fund company is willing to admit to something that all of the academic studies show to be the case, that once you get above $500 million you are going to perform in a suboptimal way. Once you get above a couple of billion it is almost impossible to outperform the averages.

John Bogle, the founder of the index fund and the most honest man in the business, has been saying this for years, but unless you are in an index fund, I know you aren't listening. You can't beat the market if you are running billions and billions of dollars. So what should an investor do? Join the market: own an index fund. If you can't find good funds that have beaten the S&P 500 for three years running, and you can't find out what that fund owns or its disposition, then what is the point? Just buy an index fund. It will give you the same return with lower fees.

The exception? I think that hedge funds, funds where the managers have their money in their funds with you and funds that allow the access I gave my investors, make sense if you can afford them. They tend to have strict requirements to determine whether you are suitable and minimum amounts that you have to invest, because the law is tougher on hedge funds. But hedge funds also have a clause that makes their structure much fairer than the mutual funds: they don't get paid unless you get paid. If a hedge fund manager loses your money in year one, he doesn't make any money in years two, three, or four until he gets you back to where you were at the start. This "high-water mark" is something that the mutual funds ought to adopt; maybe then their losses wouldn't be as staggering as they were in the bursting bubble days. I know that recommending hedge funds is antithetical to the government's wishes. But if you listen to the government about investments, you are just listening to the mutual funds and brokers, because their lobbyists rule in Washington. Hedge funds, by the way, also have to disclose when they are seeing redemptions—if they don't, they aren't telling the truth and they can get into trouble. So the most material fact to performance of mutual funds—whether they have money coming in or going out—can't be hidden in hedge funds as it is in mutual funds. The structure, while considered to be more "wild" and "unregulated" than mutual funds, is actually much more open and honest to the investor than a mutual fund, staffed for millions of investors, will ever be. It is only the mutual fund industry that has brainwashed the media into thinking otherwise. Then again, hedge funds aren't allowed to advertise, so it is no shock that they don't get a fair shake in the media and are often regarded as secretive and intensely private, when in reality it is exactly the opposite!

Why do I therefore default to index funds if you can't be in hedge funds? They have the lowest fee structure, and incur no taxes unless stocks that they own are sold for cash because they don't trade and they reinvest the dividends. You know what you own. You know what you are going to own. You can plan for the gains and losses. You aren't lied to, confused, or befuddled about size. Also, you don't have to worry about managers being switched or styles being changed, something that happens all of the time in the mutual fund industry but something that you are never told. A diversified index fund, whether it be the S&P 500 or a Total Stock Market Return fund that includes all stocks, is your best bet. That's all you can ask for from this anticlient industry.

Now, what would be an ideal portfolio? Typically, a mix of individual stocks and index funds. Unfortunately, I can't develop portfolios for everyone. People have different risk horizons and cash needs. Some are more pessimistic or optimistic. That's why anyone who tells you, Here is the ideal portfolio, without knowing you, just reveals himself as another financial mountebank.

I can tell you this, though: a mixture of five to ten stocks, well diversified with dividends, good balance sheets, coupled with an index fund that represents the S&P 500, some cash, some bonds, depending on your cash needs, and a home, which allows you the best in financial breaks—both a one-time tax break when you sell and a deduction in mortgage interest—is about the best you can do. One piece of paper, accessible to your relatives in a jiffy, that has all of your assets on it, is the best bet. Don't forget to include the value of your home and the improvements you have made to it on that piece of paper. The investment in your home will often be your biggest and best asset. Given the rapid rate with which homes have appreciated in the last several decades, that one-time avoidance of capital gains taxes (though only the first $500,000 in capital gains is exempt) on the sale of the property is a terrific windfall.

If you can't pick stocks yourself but want to do your homework, I can only advise you to watch what I am doing personally, which I make available on the Web. You can subscribe to my service, which tells you what I am buying and selling for my personal account before I do it, because I don't want you to think I am making money from you. I want you to make money from me! Why bother to listen to me rather than your broker on stocks? For starters, if your broker works at a firm that has investment banking, no matter what he says, he is compromised by his research department. Disagree? Ask him to ask any analyst at his firm to show you his yearly review. Right at the top is a question about how much value he brought to the firm's investment banking. Right at the top! Why should you listen to that person? If the firm doesn't do banking, that's different. I would defer to any analyst at such a firm who has beaten my record of 24% after all fees. Let me know who he is; I want to meet him.

Why bother to listen to me rather than journalists who have recommended portfolios in magazines and on televi-

YOU GOT SCREWED!   117

sion and in newspapers? I am not just a journalist; I am a retired pro who wants nothing more than to get you a fair
shake in your investments after watching millions of people
be bludgeoned around the head by interests that knew better but were short-term greedy instead of long-term greedy.

Above all, be skeptical. Don't be so trusting of those
whom you pay for advice. Don't be so trusting of those who
give you tips. Trust only history, the history of good managements that pay good dividends. Stop being fooled by
brokers, the media, and executives who know you only as a
mark. Start being smart about the lightweights and charlatans who never told you about the risks of stocks before you
bought them.

It is time to put an end to the rigged structure, the structure that beat you once already. I know we can do it together. Let's never get screwed again.